God for All Seasons

BOOKS BY MARLENE MAERTENS
PUBLISHED BY THE WESTMINSTER PRESS

God for All Seasons
The Challenge to the Church:
    The Niemöller-Blake Conversations (Ed.)

God for All Seasons

by Marlene Maertens

THE WESTMINSTER PRESS · PHILADELPHIA

PUBLISHED BY THE WESTMINSTER PRESS®
PHILADELPHIA, PENNSYLVANIA

PRINTED IN THE UNITED STATES OF AMERICA

SOLI DEO GLORIA

FOREWORD

This book should have been a recording. Marlene Maertens is an incomparable raconteur, and the richest impact of these Biblical and biographical narratives can be felt only when they have been heard in person. In her lifetime she has graced pulpit and podium, front porches and convention halls, chapels and cathedrals, and rarely has she failed to elicit laughter, tears, love, and respect. Now in print she is still very compelling.

Her ability to touch hearts and minds with spoken and written words is one of religious simplicity. She is in a classic way a Christian believer of profound conviction and faith, one who has heard the Word, believes the Word, loves the Word, trusts the Word, and is willing to die for the Word. And that Word is the Lord Jesus Christ, Son of the Living God.

There is something very disarming in the way Marlene Maertens tells the Story of the Word. Younger clergy, such as myself, will cast a wary eye and mind on her literal treatment and presentation of Biblical people and events. She knows all about the findings and conclusions of Biblical studies and scholarship. Yet she tells the Story of the Word with every jot and tittle intact, plus a few embellishments of her own.

However, this is not homiletical cant, nor excessive piety. She is a master storyteller and this is storytelling at its best. She knows this art form well and she uses it with the full skill and knowledge that as a vehicle for truth about God and man it is both ancient and contemporary, the classic and common means of communication for believers in every age. Thus, to leave an angel or archangel out would only violate both the medium and the message of the Story of the Word.

There is nothing precious or pristine in the way Marlene Maertens handles Biblical material. I remember once when she referred to Christmas as "the Boss's birthday." On another occasion, after reflecting upon the Gospel passage assigned for a particular Sunday she retorted about Jesus, "Boy, he sure can rub me the wrong way." Mrs. Maertens is as robust about the Bible as she is in her own life: intense, exuberant, probing, deliciously humorous, and always daring herself and others, especially ecclesiastics, to be the people of God.

Certainly that is what she is and has been, as evidenced by the biographical events she narrates in this volume. What emerges from these episodes is not the pain or sadness or loss she obviously endured, but rather the contagious joy she experienced in each instance, a joy grounded in the certainty that she was living out her own chapter in the Story of the Word. The strength and courage that that certainty gave her is always apparent. What makes these events unique is the fact that she is never surprised when the action of God occurs in her life. What we encounter is her delight when she discovers the unexpected places and people through which that action unfolds. History is both sacred and secular for Marlene Maertens. She has no desire to make artificial distinctions as to where and when the Story of the Word has or will be written. For her it is always one big and marvelous Today, God's Today.

Christmas, two years ago, Mrs. Maertens inscribed a gift copy of the Jerusalem Bible New Testament with the words, "To my favorite generation gapling." It is true that decades separate us in age, that my present work in campus ministry at a big, urban, commuter university means living the Story of the Word quite differently from the way she has lived it, and that my efforts in those movements for change in American society have in no way approximated the risks or consequences she embraced through her participation in the Confessing Church during the Nazi regime. But these differences do not constitute a discontinuity or a permanent gap between our generations. For Christians they should only mean different chapters, perhaps even different books, in the Christian Story. Marlene Maertens is right, God's Today is for real and in that setting it pleases me deeply to be her "gapling."

One of the critical problems facing all the generations today, regardless of the gaps in age, culture, and values, is the imperative task of discovering how our society can honor and revere its older members, especially those people who have that wisdom and maturity which has been tested and purified in the crucibles of adversity, pain, sacrifice, and change.

Yet change is so sudden and fast and arbitrary these days that our young people, adept and acclimated as they are to its pace and demands, are gaining experience and wisdom which in the past have almost exclusively been associated with the older generations. In fact, it is now being said that little time remains for the old to be much wiser than the young.

This should not be said with arrogance or triumph. It can be said only with dismay, because wisdom cannot be the sole possession of any generation if society as a whole is to be healthy, wise, and mature. If people grow old in America only to be regarded as irrelevant and treated with pitying tolerance, then we put dangerous time limits on maturity and wisdom which can only boomerang disastrously for young and old alike. It will mean that young people will face a future void of the very virtues they now celebrate for themselves, a celebration that inevitably will have a hollow ring when they realize that in their own agedness they will be robbed of the gracefulness and meaning and wisdom they now claim and proclaim. I cannot imagine a more tragic self-fulfilling cruelty.

No one who is truly graceful or wise or mature grows out of these qualities. They grow into them and sometimes they become them. In the Story of the Word it has been called increasing "in wisdom and in stature, and in favor with God and man." In a sense it has nothing to do with age, but it does take time. And in another sense it has nothing to do with talent or job, but it does require a total commitment in life and with life and for life.

This is what Marlene Maertens shares with us in this book: her time and commitment to the Story of the Word which in turn becomes the life of her own story. And make no mistake about it, it is graceful and wise.

EDWARD L. LEE, JR.
Episcopal Advisor
University Christian Movement
Temple University

Philadelphia, Pennsylvania

CONTENTS

FOREWORD, by Edward L. Lee, Jr.   7

INTRODUCTION   13

1. ADVENT   25

2. CHRISTMAS   37

3. EPIPHANY   54

4. LENT   72

5. GOOD FRIDAY   86

6. EASTER   96

7. PENTECOST   113

8. TRINITY   126

9. ADVENT AGAIN   146

INTRODUCTION

A book is good that presents its subject lucidly, approaches it without digression, then deals with it with care and thus becomes the record of the author's intentions. He has said what he wished to say; he envisions fertile grounds upon which his thoughts might fall. For he wishes to share them, and he hopes that his readers will feel all the richer for having read what he had to say.

These thoughts are on my mind as I realize that I cannot begin my book in such vein, in simple directness. My subject warrants an introduction that is anything but simple. It may seem diffuse, studded with too many and varying ideas. Yet I know that I should proceed as I have planned if I want to prepare the solid ground upon which my story can stand and the background to serve as an offset for the clearest possible view. I find solace in the conviction that in the long run you will find all loose ends tied up neatly.

At the outset even a brief "introduction to the Introduction" will serve to bring into focus the direction of thought set forth on the pages of this book. It consists of four comments I have recently heard or read. They are unrelated to each other but have one thing in common: they depict, or touch upon, the phenomenon of human thinking

of our day. All four lay claim to a truth as man will utter
or accept, without probing or questioning its authority,
validity, let alone its ultimate merit. Here is the first.

The other day a friend of mine and I enjoyed an ani-
mated conversation over the luncheon table. We were dis-
cussing certain points pertaining to the preparation of a
manuscript for publication. "You cannot tell people what
they should do on the pages of a book!" he said emphati-
cally. "Even if you pass on nothing but the truth, they still
don't want to read or hear it." My friend knows what he is
talking about: he is a publisher. I cannot but value his
judgment highly.

Also not long ago I spent some pleasurable hours with
a young American woman on a voyage from South Africa
to the United States. Twenty-one years old and on a world
cruise, she still displayed some signs of a carefree adolescence
but talked with sincerity about her further studies toward
a master's degree in English. One day, in equatorial waters,
we enjoyed a game of Scrabble. I was relieved to find a
spot on the board for the expensive letter "q," making the
word "qua." My young companion objected, saying that
this was a Latin word and therefore not acceptable. I agreed
to the former, but declined the latter on the grounds that
it is listed in Webster's and accepted accordingly for American usage. Politely, for she did not want to hurt my (antiquated) feelings, yet firmly, for she knew what she knew
to be the truth, she said, and not without grandeur, "Ah,
well, that may be so, but I don't care what they say and
I will not allow myself to be intimidated by a dictionary."

The third comment comes from the pen of a nationally
known columnist. He wrote about the outgoing President,
Lyndon Baines Johnson: "His weakness was that he was
too strong. Loving and believing passionately in his country,
he thought it could do anything and everything at the
same time. . . . He genuinely believed in all the great

pantings and longings and myths of his country, and was just strong enough to intimidate his associates and try to put all his dreams and yearnings into policy. It did not work but it was a good try, and the historians will probably be kinder to him than the inky wretches of the press."

Finally, another syndicated columnist wrote, in a humorous vein, as an introduction of a point he wanted to make later, "You shrink from being moralistic nowadays. . . . If you dare speak out for good against evil, millions will label you a mental antique . . . a hopeless square." And he goes on to say that now he must think up something "real real bad" about a young artist of whom he thinks highly, if he wishes to succeed in helping her on with her career.

Each of these four statements reveals a truth based on the intellectual authority of him who pronounces it, and each lays claim to be accepted as the truth by him who hears it. All four statements aim to establish some certain truth. But this truth caters to the whims, the willfulness of prevailing attitudes and workings of man's mind, ascribing the status of positivism to obvious negations in thinking. In general, man-made truths abound, flourish, and ultimately solidify the jungle of man's assertion of self as it finds interpretive expression in those Tower of Babel words "I think."

Yet there may be authority and authenticity to man's "I think," provided it flows from a different source. Provided it relates or refers to the one absolute truth, the truth from which all human truth, all workings of the human mind, must spring. It is this truth about which and in which I want to write, this truth to which I hope to witness on these pages.

This book, then, is about God the Father Almighty, Maker of heaven and earth. The Lord Jesus Christ walks through it, from the beginning to the end. And it is God the Holy Spirit causing me to write it, of this I am sure.

Were it not so, I should not dare to set about doing it.

The book is also about myself, about events and people of the very world in which we live. It then is about man with God and, in a small measure, their encounter in this world. It tells stories of such encounters and ponders over them, stories in which God speaks and acts, directs and guides in unmistakable evidence. They are told broadly, with love of detail, as such detail reveals personalities, events, and situations. They are stories of my own experience.

But it is by no means a pious book, not a collection of pious stories put together by a pious person for an "other-worldly" edification of its readers. On the contrary, it will take us into the midst of life, the thick of things, even to some places to which we cannot go today. It hopes to make relevant life on our earth today, two thousand years after Jesus of Nazareth, God-Become-Man, trod upon it, had mercy upon us, gave us the coat of his love, the directive for the way and in his person brought eternal salvation to all who believe in him, blending the Today with the Yesterday into one everlasting Forever.

This is the simple truth, not hard-to-grasp theology. We can pick it up on the pages of the Bible. And because all my stories have to do with God and God is present in the Bible, I found it appropriate to tell my stories in the context of Biblical stories, of Biblical truth. To arrange it all as orderly as I could, I chose the framework of what we call the church year, grouping my stories within the context of that season to which they are most closely related.

As to validity, I have not selected the stories depending on their locale. They occur at all sorts of places, some even inside a church. I have used the actual names of people only occasionally and with discretion, for these stories are not a revelation of self, especially not my own. Even though they happened to me, they might have happened to anybody. They might even give rise to the question, What if it had happened to me? and send the mind wandering. They differ in length, in emotion and impact, but they all say that God is everywhere. They are one in purpose, the purpose of this book: To Witness to the Living God.

We know, of course, that there is great witness evident in our world today. Just recently, in the summer of 1968, there was the great Fourth Assembly of the World Council of Churches, at Uppsala, Sweden. Nearly three thousand people had come together from all over the world, and I was one of them. This purpose gave wings to the mind as friends greeted friends and strangers from heaven knows where became friends. There was no empty sociability; there was the joy in our common faith. There was the witness in the World Council's identification with the poor, the suffering, the social evils rampant in our world today, and in the sincerity of outreach to alleviate them. For two weeks of hard work and the joy that comes from being with "our Father's business" we were encompassed in one broadly flowing stream of witness to the Living God. When we listened and prayed and sang and broke the bread of life together, it seemed as if everything in the world was utterly right and that those things which we knew were not would be righted in good time.

Yet listening to that voice within us, we had to acknowledge with sobriety that this indeed uplifting, grand witness, pleasing to the best of emotions, was the result of an organized purpose. It was indeed exciting and enriching to listen to the debates on the burning issues of our day, to watch our youth in their obvious interest and to hear what they had to say. But as some of the debates went on and on and men arose from all parts of the world to speak their mind to the point in question, we seemed to come closer and closer to those manifestations of man's "I think" as it flows, not from God, but from the national, regional, social particulars of the man presently at the microphone. This is as understandable as it is human, and often enough furnishes interesting directives. But it changes the perspective of our witness. The real witness receives its mandate by turning to God: "Lord, what wilt thou have me to do?" and in this exchange, this commitment speaks and acts no matter what the situation or problem. It is our faith in his presence with us, unseen yet real, at all times and places, that renders us truly alive and empowers us to genuine witness. Such is our part; we take it gladly even at mass meetings like the great one of Uppsala. But more so, as on the pages of this book, my witness will flow from the quiet of my heart in my home.

I love my home; it is my haven. I have come to it after erratic wanderings through a life totally thrown off course, zigzagging through extraordinary events and experiences. Not that I was born an adventurer in search of just that sort of thing; nor did I lack the desire or the directive for a well-ordered life at my husband's side: I had both, and I wanted to remain indeed where I was. But it so happened that I had to leave behind all premeditated and prearranged security, flee Germany, my native country, with my life my sole possession. This is not the place to relate the story although some parts of it recur on the pages of this book. Suffice it to say that I was found for more than one reason in a prominent place among Adolf Hitler's targets when and as his National Socialism ruled Germany. Under the impact of its laws, my life was in danger.

At this point a flashback will be helpful. Here in my room is one tangible link to the past, to my childhood and my parental roof. It is a small table with a matching three-cornered chair, of richly carved oak and more than three hundred years old. At this table my brother and I took breakfast with our father each morning, at seven o'clock sharp, for a leisurely beginning of the day. Pleasant conver-

sation was a requirement; there was no hurrying, no gulping
down of food and drink, no dashing off to school. In that
chair, at the early hour of the day, my father took pains
to instill in the minds of his young children those basic
values: punctuality, being prepared and organized for the
tasks of the day ahead. Reminiscing, as I look at the table
and chair now, the pattern of my father's educational intentions emerges clearly. He prepared his offspring for their
adult lives as responsible and respected citizens in such po-
sitions as they would attain. The sum total would be found
in well-ordered lives, well regulated in scope, emphasizing
privilege in duty and appreciation in responsibility. He left
nothing to chance, with one exception: even though grace
was said at the table, I do not recall that we really spoke
about God. By baptism and all manifestations of the Christian life we were accounted his, but in the planning, the
preparing for the secular life, God remained, even though
a given fact, yet somehow incidental.

When did it begin to dawn on me, this first faint awe,
the quiet listening, then the growing awareness that even
if I did not speak much about God, he yet spoke to me?
When did he draw a smiling line between my earnestly repeated prayers at the appointed times each day and lift me
beyond to the revelation that he speaks to me, and to all
men, constantly and by far more than we ever speak to him?

By his grace I have come to see the irrefutable truth that
God speaks to us, has spoken to us from times immemorial,
in all events that confront us, in history, through people.
By his grace alone I have come to understand that he spoke
to me, and to all men, even through National Socialism.
In all ideologies of man we clearly face the "I think" as
opposed to the faith that says "God says" and are indeed
called to make our choice, to take our stand in God's
Kingdom. The nightmare, the fight faced and suffered, are
not to be forgotten. He sanctifies the experience, leads us

through pain and anguish and humiliation to the new day in which we witness to him.

"God says": What this entails can be summarized basically and without oversimplification as "God's Law and God's Gospel." The Law: "God spake these words and said, I am the Lord thy God" and gave us the Ten Commandments, to this day the basis for the Do's and Don'ts placed before our free choice. The Gospel: "And the Word became flesh and dwelt among us, full of grace and truth; we have beheld his glory, glory as of the only Son from the Father." It is Jesus Christ, the Son, who says, "I am the Way, and the Truth, and the Life."

This is the truth from which all human truth must spring. It is so simple, we pass by without accepting it. And if we don't accept it, we can't live it; and if we don't live it, we can't witness to it. It may be best not to talk about it at all.

This is a point I find hard to understand, for I like nothing better than to talk about God, any time and place. Such conversation enlivens, enriches, elevates, and strengthens the heart to an expression of genuine worship. It places the proper values on all matters of man; it eliminates small talk and gossip. It weaves a band between the partners to such conversations; it acknowledges God to be in our midst; it makes us aware that we are members of one family who, with all their differences in structure, are yet looking out in the same direction.

This is good witness, glorifying God, wholesome to man. Such conversations can occur everywhere, just as God is everywhere. It is at this point that I want to tell the first story in Witness to the Living God. It happened at a bar. I relate it now with special joy because it found, twenty years after it happened, a fine echo at the World Council Meeting at Uppsala.

It was the time of the World Service organization; many

American churches took their place in binding the wounds of the Second World War. I was privileged to have a share in this work. My group worked out of St. Louis, Missouri. My home was a hotel room to which I returned from many assignments, from long and strenuous trips. The location of the hotel suited my needs to perfection: it was close to my office and to the railroad station; I was out far more often than in. If there was the well-known "traveling salesman" atmosphere to the place, it did not bother me, for everybody, from the manager down to the last employee, looked after my well-being and gave me the good feeling of being at home with a rather large family after all.

More often than not I would get in after eleven o'clock, exhausted from long hours of service and in real need of a bit of unwinding and some refreshment. At that hour only the bar would still be open, and, if not crowded, I would enter and take my place at the very end of it, next to the door. It was routine: David, the bartender, would greet me pleasantly, reach for a tall glass to prepare my standing order, a lemonade with lots of fruit. He usually began by giving the glass an extra polishing and, while doing so, by asking me about my work today. I always answered with special care, for David, I knew, was not a churched man.

That night there was but one other guest at the bar, over at the other end. In the quiet of the room he could not help overhearing at least fragments of what I told David of my work of that fifteen-hour day. It had to do with Displaced Persons and their relocation in this country, and I shall tell the full story in Chapter 8 of this book. David listened intently and kept polishing the glass, while I managed to get in some additional bits for him, such as looking for the one sheep that is lost or the story of the good Samaritan. As I relaxed from the strains of speechmaking followed by a vivid discussion, there was finally the well-filled glass before me.

The stranger at the other end of the bar looked up. "I
take it you are a missionary, madam?" he asked politely
enough. But he had barely finished his question when
David took him to task and with dignity called, "Sir, nobody speaks to this lady without a proper introduction!"
At that, the stranger got up, came over to my end of the
bar, and smilingly placed his calling card before me. He
was a minister of the Lutheran Church—Missouri Synod.
Well aware of the then very strong dividing line between
that denomination and others, I stretched out my hand,
told him my name, and said, "I wish we could be friends
all the way!" to which he eagerly replied, "But we can, believe me, we can and we will!"

Beginning with a discussion of denominational view-
points, our conversation was soon in full swing. He spoke
with conviction of the certainty of forthcoming changes
in the trend of thought of his church. He told of his work
as a missionary in South America, from where he had returned just now, waiting for his new assignment. He asked
about my work for World Service and I added to my reply
some of the things his own church was doing in this field
which he might not know. "Then you are a missionary
after all," he said, but I did not think that I should claim so
high a title. "That is quite wrong," he felt, "for those who
engage in the Lord's work are his missionaries, witness to
his name and ought to profess it!"

I had drained my lemonade. But David placed a fresh
glass before me without having been asked—that had never
happened before. He simply wanted the conversation to
go on, and on it went, carried by a shared conviction that
what was being said should be said. More and more the
mood of exhaustion and fatigue of two strangers who had
worked to the limit all day turned to the invigorating experience of meeting in God—and David was with us. Somehow, we both knew we would henceforth go on together,

even though on separate ways that might never cross again.

Unforgotten, the story came back to life even before I could entrust it to the pages of this book. I told it to Prof. Robert Bertram, of the Lutheran Church—Missouri Synod, the very day he addressed the great body of the World Council of Churches at Uppsala on "Our Common Christian Witness," and we were equally touched by the relevancy of the vision of my stranger-friend of twenty years ago.

Twenty years ago, God the Christ at the bar in St. Louis, helping on and blessing. And Dave, dear protective, unchurched bartender and friend, listening and listening in obvious rapture. Did something of what he heard stick? At times I have wondered.

But an answer to this question is not overly important, good though it is to have an unchurched person become sensitive to our witness. What is important is that we are, and remain, ready and willing to witness to the wonderful works of God in Christ Jesus in whom we are totally involved. We are his, are meant to be his who was yesterday, is today, and will be forever. To this truth this book shall witness, in simplicity.

1

ADVENT

Advent means "Coming," referring to the Coming of Christ. To a world in utter need, a world ever anew at the end of its rope, caught in the web of its ongoing wrongdoings, God promised his Messiah, his Christ. Mankind was longing for him. He would liberate. He would set free. He would come and be among them, he would be right here and take leadership.

In the blending of time and eternity into one great Today, the final wait for Christ's arriving became the Advent season, for more than twelve hundred years now commonly accepted as the beginning of the church year by all Christendom. Mankind within God's eternal circle, from Advent to Advent Again: Christ coming into the world to redeem it; and Christ coming again, at the end of time, to judge both the quick and the dead. We do not know when that will be: we live today.

We must think about these things, must define them for our own understanding. We must apply their meaning to our own life and to the life of man Today. To do this is not the assigned task or the prerogative of the specialists, of theologians and historians, nor is it the prerogative of any one church alone. It is a God-given challenge to all men to identify themselves as belonging to him, as being a part of him. It is both challenge and privilege to all Christians who witness to him with their lives because he gave it.

For twelve centuries we have commemorated the Advent season as the beginning of the church year; we still do it today. This very fact merits, in our time of rapid changes, a probe into the meaning of Advent in its relevance to us, to life Today. To all who are alive, Today is all-important. Today—what is Today?

Today, in some measure, appears to be a peak between yesterday and tomorrow. Webster's defines the word as "the present day, time, or age." It means the date, the day, the month, the year. Today denotes some special event, a birth, a death, an anniversary. Today's weather is a case in point. Today good things are happening and bad things also and they become a part of that day's record. Today, man's mind explores new fields of science, creates new wonders, helps man to live with an artificial heart; today, man finds out how to mushroom the world into oblivion or look upon her from the moon. Today is the scene of untold human activity, covering the full range of man's capacities and emotions. Man even transfers the intricacies of his mind to a set of myriads of wires and wheels and electronics to see a machine give printed answers to the questions it is fed. Today, we bend over backward to gaze beyond the destruction of the mushroom cloud into outer space; today, at our feet there are civil rights and poverty and Vietnam and other hostilities. Today, people still kill people, calling it a holy war.

Of course there is also our Today of peace-seeking and peace-making and of earnest efforts undertaken in faith, not to be overcome by evil but to overcome evil with good. Such is the string of our Todays that become Yesterday as we add a new one Tomorrow.

But then there is God's Today, that one Today which changes not. It is as comprehensive, as all-inclusive, as the

Creation itself of which it is a part. To comprehend this, God's Today, means to acknowledge him as who he is: the Creator, the Father of us all, ruling supreme over his Creation in perpetual activity. To this truth we attune our bodies, hearts, and minds and take all life from there, only from there. But this is precisely where man has trespassed from the beginning of his existence. He has trespassed, and still does so today, on his place in the Creation. He has always confused, or refused to accept, the inescapable fact that he is the creature, not the creator. This is the root of man's alienation from God, his Maker, without whom he can never truly live.

Today then is the reality of the story of the Garden of Eden. Man and woman, the ultimate in God's creating, are placed together in the fullness of paradise. They know neither need nor want. They are given dominion over the earth and all that is therein. They are blessed by God and encouraged to activity. Within the setting of perfect peace, they receive but one veto: "You may freely eat of every tree in the garden; but of the tree of the knowledge of good and evil you shall not eat, for in the day that you eat of it you shall die."

You shall die: God left no doubt, he neither said nor indicated a "maybe." From the beginning, his voice has been strong, his command clear. He asserts himself as the Creator. Having given all, he can also take all. The binding action is his. He blesses and he punishes. Adam, Eve, the serpent—all have disobeyed his command, have reached up to the level of equality with God himself, just as we still are doing today.

I have sometimes wondered what might have happened had they but found a simple, "O Lord, forgive us." We do not know, and they did not find it. Instead, the man attempts to rid himself of his share in the guilt. He tries to lay the blame on someone else—on Eve, "the woman";

then even on God himself, "whom thou gavest to be with me"; and on to the serpent. God drives them out of paradise, into the world of toil and tribulation, and of death. He closes the gate, places a guard, the cherubim with a flaming sword, and thus affirms the Creator's unquestionable rule over his Creation.

The story is no less authentic now than it was then. It is as relevant as it is obvious. Man Today still does not accept the word of God, neither heeds nor lives by it. He disregards and disobeys God more often than not, he does not take him seriously. He may, at times, interpret the word of God to suit his own aims, which is another version of setting himself in God's place. The results are all about us. They look as if taken directly from the pages of the Old Testament. Yes, we are in a world of toil and tribulation, and of death. We are not in paradise. But we still know of the paradise, we are still near it, for God did not stay behind the fast closed gate. He came along with us. He is with us Today.

Today is the reality of the story of Cain and Abel. Man's disobedience of God produces a new facet: Cain's unwillingness to accept God's free choice, his actions, his judgment over man's accomplishment. The husbandman and the shepherd, hardworking brothers both. They are dedicated to their chores, the yield of the fields, the growth of the flock. They bring their burnt offering before God. Yet at this time it is Abel's sacrifice, not Cain's, that finds favor with God. Cain sulks, he gets mad. "Why are you angry," God asks, "and why has your countenance fallen? If you do well, will you not be accepted? And if you do not well, sin is couching at the door; its desire is for you, but you must master it."

But Cain does not want God's lesson. And so, for disappointment turning to anger, and envy to hatred, Cain kills his brother. He feels no responsibility. He does not think he is his brother's keeper, and he tells God so. And ever since, and indeed for the same motives, brother has continued to kill brother down to this day, in more ways than one.

The story does not end here; it flows into the Today throughout the ages. Cain, the fratricide, goes forth into a world of his own. He becomes a husband, a father, the ancestor of generations of the growing population on earth. With them, civilization begins. From its beginning we can observe, faintly at first but growing stronger, the dividing line between those people who live with God, or try to live with God, and those who do not, who live believing in the authority of their own prudence. Cain is the link, Cain with God's mark of the murderer on his forehead; Cain who "went away from the presence of the Lord," as we assuredly do today. Yet even there, Cain is not left alone; the Lord God yet goes with him, just as he did with Adam and Eve, Cain's parents. The Creator stays with his creature; he protects him from being murdered and thus ordains the basic directive for all eternity for his children on earth: "Mine is the vengeance, I will repay," says the Lord.

Yes, God punishes Adam and Eve; he punishes the serpent; and now he punishes Cain. In other words, he punishes the individual for his immediate sin. But now, as mankind expands to multitudes of people, there is a significant difference. God deals with the multitudes as they consist of individuals. And Today, as we disobey God and sin against him as individuals within the multitude, so do we sin as the multitude of which we are a part.

Today then is the dreadful reality of the story of the Tower of Babel. In our relationship with God, here is the event of jolting impact, of the deepest significance yet for the life of man, the individual and his community. We are challenged to make up our mind. We are challenged to make the choice between acknowledging God as the Creator who rules over our community and is worshiped accordingly, and elevating the self as the creature of our own making and rule—and live and worship the creature rather than the creator accordingly. We come face to face with idolatry.

The people who built the Tower of Babel chose the latter. The story tells of mankind, living together now as one great family. They are tuned in upon each other, they enjoy it and they speak, literally and figuratively, the same language. One senses their exuberance, their enthusiasm at doing things. We read of the acquired skill of their hands, the brilliancy of keen minds. As they wander about, they select a site for a city for themselves, a city to be built with an enormous tower to reach up to heaven and to protect them and keep them together. "Let us make a name for ourselves," this thought was their driving power. They went to work. Keen minds created the blueprint and skilled hands began to make bricks.

It is difficult, if not impossible, to decide which is the greater evil, the thought or the deed. It is a question our own era faces daily anew. It remains difficult, if not impossible, to extricate the multitudes busily building the tower under the command of their taskmasters and pronounce them free of guilt. The crux of the matter remains: all of the people involved in building the Tower of Babel knew that they trespassed upon God's domain: their tower in their city would reach up unto heaven. City and tower were meant to make "a name for ourselves." Again, the creature sets himself above the Creator, again he reaches up to equality with God. City and tower are to be a monument to man's mind. In his outreach man competes with God instead of seeking God's inspiration and asking his blessing upon his plans and the work of his hands.

In this story, thought and deed are inextricably intertwined: all become guilty of sinning against the supremacy of God. Again the Lord God asserts himself. He no longer punishes the individual. He does not take to task the architect or the contractor or the foreman of the laborers. He extends his punishment to all alike; together they share it, just as before they had shared his blessing of prosperity. It is a hard lesson, not to grasp, but to accept; our own Today is one big example of revolting against it as we go on worshiping the creature over the creator and as we refuse to bear together what is coming to us according to God's ways, be it punishment, be it even blessing.

The punishment for the building of the Tower of Babel is tremendous. God comes down, so the story says, and confounds it all. He confounds man's mind and he confounds man's language, and he scatters him all over the earth. And even though we, knowing more than they knew then, may see his rainbow of forgiveness over all his doings, and may turn the leaf over and in his name begin anew, yet have to stop to face a fact. That fact cannot be understood clearly enough. The confounding of man's mind and man's language does not mean the birth of peoples and different languages as we have them today and all through man's history. No, to this day it means the terror of brother sitting with brother and friend with friend; they talk and talk but do not understand what the other fellow is talking about. We have to work at understanding and being understood, no matter how big, no matter how small the subject might be. Even the shape of a conference table may be interpretive both of the confusion and the work involved to cut through the confusion!

Thus, flowing in our Today, nonunderstanding, misunderstanding, misconception, and misinterpretation pave the ugly road to enmity and its crowning triumph: war, destruction, and death. It is God's punishment for man's deification of himself.

"Now this is not nice of God!" a friend of mine ex-

claimed in Bible class one night not long ago, and several
members of the group sided with her in great dismay. Her
remark was typical of the thoughts of so many of us still
holding on to the snug shelter of our organized churchian-
ity. Yet as they began to probe deeper, she, and the other
members of our group, touched on the very point in question. Friendly people, intelligent, faithful members of their
church, they merely expressed man's longing for the paradise and decline to admit that it is lost. They think Cain
should not have slain his brother, because they are sure
they would not slay their own brother either. They, and
all of us, fail to identify themselves with those eternal
examples of God's choosing, fail to see that we act like they
did, act like they did in numbers, that we are God's creatures, his children, as they were, that their Today is our
Today. And safe in the protective folds of our churches we
go on stepping unwittingly and unwillingly across the dis-
tinction between the Creator and his creature, this dividing
line which from the beginning God has drawn so con-
clusively. Also from the beginning, man has matched God's
act by refusing to recognize, acknowledge, accept, and mind
it. Yet with customary devotion we repeat it in church quite
earnestly, this "In his hands are all the corners of the
earth, and the strength of the hills is his also."

I have dwelt on God's punishment for man's transgres-
sions hopefully no longer, no more severely than is necessary
to have it conscientiously incorporated in our Today. Of
course this Today is also the reality of all that is good, the
beauty of the earth, the people who strive to live with God.
Our Today is indeed the reality of the stories of scores of
God-loving, God-fearing men who knew themselves and
their destiny in his hands and took life from there. From
among great numbers of men on the pages of the Old
Testament and through the ages we think of his obedient
servants. We think of Noah, Abraham, Moses, Joshua, of
myriads of people who have become our example for man's

faith and his obedience to God. We think of Job, who amid
dire tribulation yet accepted God's rule and welcomed it.
We let Joshua, Moses' successor as the leader of the children of Israel, express for us that focal point of our Today
as he gave it to God's chosen people of the Old Testament:
"Choose you this day whom ye will serve; whether the gods
which your fathers served that were on the other side of
the flood, or the gods of the Amorites, in whose land ye
dwell: but as for me and my house, we will serve the Lord."

We are comforted to realize that God knows us as we
are; we hold no surprises for him. Call it sin, call it weakness, sum up the record of man failing God: it is by reaching for godlikeness that man has fallen into ungodliness.
From the beginning, this has been our Today, and God has
never failed to deal with it. But even in his greatest wrath,
his severest punishment, his yet unsearchable action has
sprung, and still does, from but one source: his love for
his own creature. And so, as we draw up a balance sheet of
our status Today, we find many people among us who serve
God as Joshua and his house once did. But we must also be
aware of the sum total of our failures, our sins. Today,
embraced by the extremes from self-deification to apathy,
man is in dire need of God, the God of whom we read on
the pages of the Old Testament and whom we really come
to know much later.

But we do not like it much to read that book and make
it our own. It is understandable: we do not like to read our
own story all over again, enacted by different people under
different circumstances at a different time. Through the
centuries we have tried to disregard it; better still: to ignore
it and warm ourselves in an approving acceptance of the
New Testament. Between the first and the twentieth century, from Marcion to Adolf Hitler, there is hardly the
need to fix the blame. An examination of our own stand
will generally do. We may reach for the Old Book. It does
not take long till we are bored with those many repetitions,

the endless genealogies, the references to a civilization and culture not our own. Yet we need those patient repetitions of God's stories because we never listen the first time around. We are the offspring of those endless genealogies. Civilization and culture? Too long ago to be of interest. We are proud of our own. We are people of taste and refinement, advanced in knowledge. We are above those bloodthirsty stories, these tales of conquest; we are above the deceit and revenge some of those old stories so amply display. But above all, we are above crime and war.

Or are we? Yet we pretend more often than not that we have nothing in common with those old Jews, the Children of Israel, God's chosen people. We are Christians, are we not? Yes, we are: Christians at the crossroad of lip service and yearning to advance to the real thing on God's hand. Christians who acknowledge the origin of their sin and its ongoing factualness. Christians who take their place in God's Today and wait for him.

To us, his fallen race, God promised, and ultimately sent, his Messiah. Yet God's Messiah, the Lord Jesus Christ, is not some new beginning: he is the fulfillment of God's Law, the expression of God's love. He is the Word of God; in him rests all of God's Today.

Yet this ultimate Today cannot become the reality of the Advent of Christ unless we firmly accept the reality of the Old Testament within us. Unless we acknowledge our kinship with these sinning, erring, loving, faithful, warring, peaceful people. Unless we show some pride and identify ourselves with those great men who heard the word of God, kept and tried to live by it. To all of them, to sinner and righteous alike, God promised his Messiah. This is the eternal truth, this is our truth Today. This is what we must understand and accept wholeheartedly. Then, and only then, are we ready in faith for God's promised gift, the Advent of his Christ.

The story I am about to offer in this context is particularly dear to me because little Herbie, its hero, was prepared for the Advent of Christ without knowing it. I met him when he was all of seven years old, in a Home for Children in Missouri. He was a cheerful little fellow with a ready smile, but once you looked into his eyes deeply enough you could see the bewilderment, the pain of the unwanted, unloved, uncared-for child. He came from a setting of horror, where hapless people top one wrong with another, inflicting the ever-widening circle of their own misery upon all within their reach, especially their children. With the gutter for his nursery, young Herbie at first sight betrayed no signs of injury or damage to his mind. He seemed to relish his new environment where he had been brought to grow up wanted, loved, and cared for, with nearly one hundred brothers and sisters from similar "broken homes," as we put it politely.

My job was the Home's public relations work. It took me all over the state to tell about the children, their life, their needs. It kept me on the road most of the time, but when I was at the Home I tried to learn as much about each child as possible and to understand the atmosphere in which they lived.

On one of those Home days, a member of the staff asked me to give the devotions the following morning at the breakfast table. The children would enjoy a change in their daily fare, or so he thought. But as I did not fully share the daily life of the Home, I wondered what special offering I could make. My final choice came from the conviction that nothing speaks to us as clearly, as lovingly and helpfully, as God himself. Accordingly, I put together a few selections from the Bible, such as I hoped would find a permanent place in those young hearts and minds.

I began with the Twenty-third Psalm, reciting it slowly so that King David with God would be felt in our midst. I continued with another brief passage from the Old Testament and then let the thirteenth chapter of Paul's first letter to the Corinthians ring out. After the last verse I added one more quotation from the New Testament. My little congregation listened attentively. They arose; we repeated the Lord's Prayer together. That was the end.

The children filed out of the dining room to begin their day at school or play. Some had a quick "hello" for me or a special greeting. As I gathered my books and papers for an imminent departure, I noticed one small youngster coming slowly toward me. His brown eyes were aglow, full of purpose. I stretched out my hand and smiled at him. "Hello, Herbie." I waited. A deep sigh, and then, "Oh, that was beautiful," and another deep sigh. "What did you like especially, Herbie?" The seven-year-old answered as best he could and quite reluctantly. "Well," he said, "there was something about understanding . . ." "Would you like to hear it again?" I suggested. He nodded vigorously. And this child of God looked into the Book while I held the finger to the text and read very slowly: "Wisdom is the principal thing; therefore get wisdom: and with all thy getting get understanding!"

"Is that it, Herbie?" I asked, and again he nodded vigorously. But he remained close to me and made no move to be on his way. Finally, he looked at me directly, his eyes pools of radiance. "Well," he said, "you said something else. It was at the end, and it was beautiful . . . the most beautiful thing . . ." His voice trailed off.

Once again I opened the Bible and read for young Herbie "the most beautiful thing" he wanted to hear again:

For God so loved the world that he gave his only Son, that whoever believes in him should not perish but have eternal life.

Herbie, young offspring of Cain, was ready for Advent.

2
CHRISTMAS

To the fallen race, doomed in the thoughtlessness of continuous sin, God came. We know the story; we have read it many times. It never fails to touch us deeply, to stir our emotions and our sense of joy. From generation to generation, it sustains our sense of tradition, this cherished reading at Christmas, the story of the birth of Christ, as Luke tells it. It draws us to the manger at Bethlehem; we gaze and we marvel. We hear the angels sing, and we sing right along with them. Joy to the world, the Lord is come!

But reading and hearing and marveling are one thing, while understanding and retaining and putting to use are a different matter. The Christian living God's Today is called upon to do both. While it is not difficult to exclaim in exultation, "Christ the Savior is born!" it takes the response of a searching mind to grasp the divine Love made manifest, the Light that came to shine in the darkness, and the Life Eternal come to man in Christ.

Beautiful reading as Luke's account of the birth of the Savior is, it yet remains a factual report, and rather scarce at that. It simply tells of Caesar Augustus' decree concerning the taxation of his peoples and the directives to be followed. It tells of Joseph of Nazareth who had to leave his residence in Nazareth (Galilee) and go to Bethlehem

(Judea) to oblige the law. It tells that he had to take his
wife along, Mary, who expected the birth of her first child.
It briefly refers to the hardships involved in that trip; then
the child is born, his crib a manger. This is contained in
thirteen lines of reading in the book in which I read it over
just now. It takes another thirteen lines to describe the
spectacular events following the birth of the child and connected with it. It rises beyond a simple narrative as it
proclaims the heavenly participation: "Fear not: for, behold, I bring you good tidings of great joy, which shall be
to all people. For unto you is born this day in the city of
David a Savior, which is Christ the Lord." And we join with
the multitude of the suddenly appearing heavenly host,
singing, "Glory to God in the highest, and on earth peace,
good will toward men."

A lifetime is just long enough to ponder over the story
of the birth of Christ, to contemplate its impact on our life,
on all life on earth Today. I think that we miss something
very important unless we relive the story over and over
again. Unless we see it before our mind's eye, for, as the
saying goes, that which the eye sees, the mind will retain
forever.

I can see that carpenter shop in Nazareth, Joseph bent
over his work, a neighbor stopping by. "Joseph, does this
decree concern you?" "It does," answers the quiet man
without stopping to work, "and we shall have to go to
Bethlehem." "We?" asks the neighbor. "Mary in her con-
dition?" "Yes," Joseph says. "Mary shall go with me," and
as an afterthought, "I shall try to make it as comfortable
for her as I can."

I can see them, Joseph and Mary, getting ready for the
long trip, quietly obedient to the law of the land. I can
see Joseph handing over his shop and all the tools to a
friend and trusted caretaker; I can see Mary packing her
bundles and one very special one: the things for her ex-

pected child. I can see the little donkey being charged with their belongings—as they close their home and say farewell to the neighbors.

I can see them setting out on the long and dusty road, the tall man and the gentle woman, Joseph and Mary of Nazareth, with their little donkey carrying their belongings. There is a last stop for a drink of fresh water at their city's well; they replenish their supply, they chat with friends who are there drawing their need for the day. I can see them looking back once more upon their city, a poor little village by our standards today. To them it was home, those small houses, whitewashed and square, with flat roofs and a bit of greenery here and there.

To them it was home, and they were about to leave it at a time when they should have most liked to stay—for how long they did not know. On the top of the hill, before the final bend of the road, they took a parting view of their landscape, the city on its hill, Lake Galilee deep down in the distance and, beyond the River Jordan, the peaks of Mt. Hermon, as if touching the clouds. To the other side, to the west, beyond the horizon, there was the Great Sea.

They may have enjoyed both vision and wideness, but now they faced their tedious task. Slowly they started out downhill on the narrow road, not built for Roman cohorts on the march but trampled down by the hooves of flocks in search of food. Downhill step by laborious step, the quiet man and the pregnant woman, till they reached the big plain with its vineyards, its gardens and pastures. How much enjoyment did they have, how much rest? What did they think, what did they talk about? I am sure their minds were now preoccupied with one purpose: to reach Bethlehem as fast as possible.

On they went, climbing another hill and going down again, obediently, dutifully, through that strange land called Samaria, into Judea, through the golden city, Jerusalem, and on and on till they finally reached their destination, the little town of Bethlehem.

There were no kinfolk left to welcome them to their home. They went to the inn, but there was no room available. That was to be expected, as under the Emperor's decree a great many people had to travel to their place of origin just like Joseph, and the age of hotel reservations was far in coming. But the innkeeper did by them as best he could. He took one look at the beautiful young woman being so great with child. He had just the right place, a place of privacy and seclusion. It would be warm and dry and comfortable—a shelter, to be sure. It may have been a stable, or a cave hewn into the rocks and connected with the inn. At any rate, they shared it with some friendly animals, and so did God's first man and woman in paradise.

This then, in Bethlehem, the royal city of Joseph's forebear King David, is where our weary travelers found rest. It was not merely the physical stress and strain of the trip. There was much more to it. How lonely they must have been amid the many travelers on the road! They shared the same fate, but their thoughts set them apart from all other human beings. For even while he watched over Mary's comfort every step of the way, Joseph had time enough to contemplate over and over again that which he had heard and seen in his dream: "Joseph," an angel of the Lord said to him, "Joseph, son of David, do not fear to take Mary your wife, for that which is conceived in her is of the Holy Spirit; she will bear a son, and you shall call his name Jesus, for he will save his people from their sins!"

When Joseph woke from his sleep, he remembered what the Lord had spoken by the prophet: "Behold, a virgin shall conceive and bear a son, and his name shall be called Emmanuel" (which means "God with us"). Joseph did as the angel of the Lord commanded him. He took his wife but knew her not until—until her son would be born. This time had now come.

Joseph, the just man, lived a life with God. He believed, he was obedient and carried out what he was charged to do. It shines through him, through all we know of him: he lived a simple life of love.

And Mary? Who can fathom her thoughts, her feelings, as quietly she recalled the things that had happened to her? Now that her hour had come, that she could rest from the trip and for her great task ahead, she let it all pass over her mind again. She remembered the depth of her confusion at the appearing of her strange visitor. He was a messenger from God who had come to tell her that God had singled her out, had blessed her among women. She did not understand what it meant. The messenger said that she was to conceive and bear a son whom she was to call Jesus. He would be great and called the Son of the Highest. God himself would give him the throne of David, he would reign over the house of Jacob forever; his Kingdom would never end.

As she mastered her bewilderment, Mary had something to say, too. She did not say, "I don't believe this, this is foolish, this is unrealistic." She had one simple question: "How can I have a child, since I have no husband?"

The angel's answer was not easy to grasp. He lifted her up to the reality of God's plan for the redemption of his children on earth, brought her face to face with the prophecies of old: God's Messiah would be born of a virgin. God had chosen her to be this virgin. His Holy Spirit would cause this child to come to life in her body and be born of her. And, as if wanting to help her along in understanding, he took her back to her own little world. He told her that her cousin Elizabeth, advanced in years and known to be barren, had also conceived a son. He would be born about six months before her son, Jesus. . . . Yes, she remembered that it had been very bewildering, even as she recalled it now.

But Mary knew what to do with bewilderment, with

fright, with seemingly unanswerable questions. She placed it all, and herself with it, at the feet of God. "Behold the handmaid of God," she said gently. "Be it unto me according to thy word."

"Thy word." Mary knew that it was God's word. Believing, obedient, full of faith, Mary welcomed the Word of God in her mortal body.

She remembered her visit with her cousin Elizabeth. She was with child, as the angel had said. But Elizabeth greeted her in a most unusual way. It was obvious that she knew the high purpose for which her young cousin had been selected. "Blessed art thou among women," she cried, "and blessed is the fruit of thy womb!" And Mary, holding very very still to the impact of this moment, professed:

> My soul does magnify the Lord,
> And my spirit has rejoiced in God my Savior.
> For he has regarded the lowliness of his handmaiden:
> For, behold, from henceforth
> All generations shall call me blessed.
> For he that is mighty has magnified me;
> And holy is his name.

We do not know, and we need not know, whether Mary, who became the wife of Joseph of Nazareth, fully grasped the part God had chosen her to take. Humbly, faithfully, obediently, she accepted. She said Yes to God, and that means that she lived a life of simple love.

In the dark of the night, the Son was born. She tended to his needs. She wrapped him in the swaddling clothes she had brought along. She placed him in a little manger, neatly filled with straw. She made him comfortable.

Quietly, Joseph sustained her. Steeped in his thoughts, he watched over the young mother and her Child.

In the dark of the night, the sky began to shine. It sparkled with stars; it resounded with celestial sound. In the dark of the night, a radiant message made itself known. Some shepherds in the field, keeping watch over their flock, were the ones to see and hear it. This was no vision. This was real, this was God revealing himself! They were benumbed with fear! But God had an angel tell them not to fear, for here was reason for great joy, joy for all people:

For unto you is born this day in the city of David a Savior, which is Christ the Lord!

The Savior? God's promised Messiah for whom the people had longed for generations? Was this true?

The angel reassured them. "Go and see the babe," he called. "He is wrapped in swaddling clothes, lying in a manger!"

They were totally bewildered, dumbfounded. Christ the Lord, a Savior, a babe in a manger, in the city of David?

They were not left alone in their thoughts. Then and there, before their very eyes and round about them, the sky opened up, heaven and earth blended into one, God's creation aflame with light, resplendent with celestial glory. A host of angels singing, praising God, ascribing all glory to him, yet leaving with mortal man the eternal challenge, "And on earth peace, good will toward men!"

The spectacle faded; the night was dark and still again, the flock asleep. The stars sparkled as before, remote, beyond man's reach. One very bright one stood over Bethlehem. The shepherds saw it. They recovered from the excitement, from their fear. God had revealed himself to them. They lost no time now. They hurried to Bethlehem to find the babe in the manger.

A group of shepherds, unwashed and unkempt, simple folk from the country, were the Christ-child's first visitors. They looked at him; they bent their knees. God had spoken. God had acted. The Savior was born and this is what he looked like: a babe in a manger. They accepted it.

They worshiped. They left. But they praised God as they went forth, and they shared all they had heard and seen with all who were willing to listen and to accept the divine truth from a human mouth.

"For God so loved the world that he gave his only Son . . ." In Love, God manifested himself. The Light in the darkness: God's love. The new Life in Jesus Christ: God's love. The Babe in the manger of Bethlehem, Jesus the Christ, tended by quietly loving parents, first worshiped by rough, uneducated shepherds, sent there by God himself, is God's Light, Love, and Life to our man-made darkness Today.

I love to ponder these things, particularly at Christmas, of course. I have been alone that night of nights for many years now and have come to thank God for the unique privilege more often than not to be found in solitude. As I light my South Carolina bayberry candles grouped around the little tree from Minnesota, I can send my thoughts where they most want to be. I can truly relive the reality of the Coming of God in its timeless meaning: God coming to us, God being with us, God remaining with us to the end of time—to ransom our souls. I can associate these thoughts with the tiny crèche before my eyes, a precious piece of art, hand-carved at Oberammergau. I can read Luke's story from my Bible, my companion of more than thirty event-filled years. I read it to myself, to the walls, and through them to all the world. I read it with my eyes closed, to see it with my mind, and I know it will never leave me again.

It is an hour of an unbelievable Oneness with God, the Creator, with his creation and all his creatures, in and through Jesus Christ. For thirty years now I have come to cherish the solitude that makes this experience possible. It provides the setting to attune to the significance upon all life of God's gift: God's love come to man in Christ Jesus.

Let it be said: this is not a record of an aging person's deep emotions and not a characterization of one being "too enthusiastic, too superlative." In the contrary, and I want to put it this way: I feel cold-soberly that no enthusiasm, no superlative of human making, can match the overwhelming simplicity of God's invitation, "Go to the manger and see the child and bend your knee and believe in him." We need the courage to profess to enthusiasm and superlative, in order to grasp the truth: the darker the night about us, the brighter shines God's message. He will be with us through our life of recurring sin, he has put the coat of his love around our shoulders.

To come to know all this means that we have to witness to it. It is not personal property. This knowledge, this love, has to be shared. We let it flow on through us to others. We want to be known by it, by God's love. And not in pious words without substance, not solely in our life at church, but in attitude, outlook, outreach; in willingness to be of service where service is needed.

And, indeed, in prayer. My solitary Christmas is crowned by it. But strange as it may sound, I am the one who derives an immediate blessing of peace and joy. As I have read the story, repeated it in my native tongue in which I first knew it, I look into the softly glowing candles, the tiny crèche. I close my eyes and let my thoughts go. They stop at my neighbors, they go on unhurriedly from person to person in my life just as they come to mind. They may live down the street or on the other side of the globe, my thoughts will find them. This last Christmas, they went out to three men circling the moon. Yes, time and space lose their significance even for me, lose their claim upon life on this loved journey. The thought, "Now whom have I forgotten?" has not occurred yet; it is the most natural thing to do, to think of everybody in the love of God in Christmas. It is wonderful then to go on thinking of the others whom

I do not know and to stretch out my hand holding God's love. It is the greatest experience I know, this my solitary Christmas in God with all mankind, the very blessing of peace and joy.

Of course there are other forms of Christmas; some of these shall now be taken under scrutiny to clear the way for our thinking. No, I do not intend to dwell on an ever-expanding commercialism that makes a public farce of mankind's paramount gift. Somewhere within that friendly madness of printed cards and parties and gifts there is still the clear trace of love which prompts these activities, even unto total exhaustion. The relief is in sight: "As soon as Christmas is over . . ."

No, I want to speak of the terrible distortions of Christmas which undo God's purpose and deface the gift. I shall do that by offering a story of contrasts. It starts out gently enough, referring to the first thirty years of my life in my native country, Germany. Through childhood, adolescence, and young womanhood Christmas remained indeed the shared experience of God's love, translated into beauty, gladness, gratitude, contentment, and giving. Steeped in tradition, it was awaited year after year in the same happy anticipation. A lovely Advent season, in itself rich in special customs, gave cause for much visiting among families and friends, all busy with preparations for Christmas, the Coming of the Christ-child. If generalization is possible, and for once permissible, it may indeed apply here to the way in which an entire people prepared and then held its Christmas.

In the early afternoon of December 24, called the "Holy Evening," shops, restaurants, movies, theaters, closed down. Only the essentials to public life were kept functioning. The people went home.

When darkness fell, a stillness enveloped the country which my words cannot describe. By five o'clock, the bells of the churches would ring and the family, the entire household, would go to church together in silence. From the moment the doors opened, the church would be packed, packed as one big family who were gathering for the same purpose: to celebrate the birth of the Savior. In my home church, the altar was flanked by two enormous Christmas trees, each bedecked with three hundred wax candles (we were given this unbelievable number in confirmation class). Year after year, the service followed the same order of worship. It was very simple; there was no liturgy, no sermon. We sang, we listened, we prayed, and we sang some more. From the altar, Luke's story was read, read as though he who read it and we who heard it heard it for the first time in our life, yet never to be forgotten again. It was read in three parts, and each part was framed by appropriate, century-old carols and cradle songs. We had no crèche in our church, but we were at the manger indeed. We praised and glorified God with enthusiasm, we were all rich beyond measure. We sang the closing hymn in exultation: it praises the glad, the blessed, Christmas season; speaks of a lost world into which Christ was born, born to redeem us. The church bells pealed along with our singing; we knew what we were celebrating. It was utterly beautiful, forever unforgettable. As quietly as we came, we went home to the family Christmas held, of course, according to one's own and cherished tradition.

The following two days were the First and the Second Christmas Day, national holidays both. They were observed by traditional solemn worship services in a festive mood but church-directed fashion.

I have told this rather broadly, not just because I love to tell about it but more so because I want to bring into focus the distortion of Christmas in Germany under the new rule. From one Christmas to the next, things changed radically. National Socialism, the new ideology which many called the new gospel, was planted among and forced upon us. Its concept of life, its teachings, its manifestations in everyday living, amounted to a new upsurge of unabashed deification of man, based upon man's blood and his race. Beyond doubt, beyond even a possibility of adjustment or compromise, the ideology of the deification of man in National Socialism was the exact opposite to God's Word-Become-Flesh in the Child of Bethlehem.

It was only natural that Christmas, with its time-honored traditions of an entire people, with its unifying appeal, provided an excellent entry for the revival of pagan thought. Weihnachten, those sacred nights in Germanic folklore, when lights upon the trees in the forest pointed the way to the wanderer, when Wotan and his lesser gods were about, when valiant friendships were sealed with armed might. This was the kind of heroism we now were after. It interpreted National Socialist thinking; it called the people away from that lowly manger of Bethlehem in the land of the Jews. It did not take long to come out into the open: Weihnachten was declared a Germanic festival embracing all Germans in the wide world. We may not call this ecumenical love. This love was for Germans only.

I think of another distortion of Christmas, in yet another country, the Republic of South Africa. It is a land of paradiselike beauty, and I hope and pray that this great beauty will be reflected, one of these days, in all that this country does.

South Africa is in the southern hemisphere; it is summer at Christmas, and nature breaks forth in a riot of color and blossoms. I spent this Christmas with dear friends on their farm not far from Johannesburg. We had a few pieces of traditional Christmas greens, because there was one Douglas fir on the land. But the mainstay for decorating the house were hundreds of dark red roses which we picked early in the morning fresh with dew. We combined them with

candles of the same dark red color in all sorts of arrangements. It was a feast for the eye, expressed our mood, ap-
pealed to the emotions.

At the appointed hour, we gathered in the big living
room. Our host reached for the Bible and read the beloved
story we all knew. He read it to us who were in that room.
He had to leave that room and read the story again, to the
servants on the farm, native Africans who under the law of
the land were not permitted to be one with us in that room.
I remember the thought that passed my mind then. It was:
The shepherds are refused admittance!

Yet I firmly believe that God's love prevails and rules, no
matter what we do. If we dwell too long, too hard on the
failures of man, we might even overlook the magnitude of
God's love exemplified in people, in the things they do,
and in events. With these manifestations of God's love in
Christ Jesus in mind, I have chosen to tell the story now
following.

From the beginning, the story impressed me as somewhat
unreal, a mystery. One night late in 1943 my telephone
rang after I had fallen asleep. "I hope I have not disturbed
you calling so late," the pleasant voice of my friend Jeanette
said. With apparent excitement she went on to say that she
had spent the evening with a group of women of her
church. They were planning a special event to be held right
after the first of the year, but still within the Christmas
season. A sudden pause, her voice trailed off.

They want me for a speaker, I thought to myself,
wondering why Jeanette did not come right out with it,
for I knew her to be a straightforward person. "Well," she
continued with some hesitancy showing, "what we are
planning is an international night," and at that her voice
trailed off as before. "Jeanette," I wondered, "International
Night at Christmas during war?" and a terrifying thought
crept up within me.

"Well," here was the pleasant voice again, "this is exactly what we have in mind. Because of Christmas, because of the war, we want to do something to signify the family of man under God and that is why we want you to represent Germany on this program. We know you can do it!"

I caught my breath. This could not be possible. It was 1943, the United States at war with Germany, and I, classified as an Enemy Alien, was to represent that country to the Women's Guild of St. Luke's Church in Louisville, Kentucky.

I did not want to refuse her outright. "Who else will be on that program?" I asked to smooth the confusion on my mind. "We hope to get quite a few to serve," Jeanette assured me. "We already have two women from England and France—" "And they'll be thrilled to serve together with me?" I could not help interrupting her. But she went right on: "We'll have Lu Cheng Hao from China. And Ilona, who will wear her Hungarian costume—she looks lovely in it. And I shall try to get some more representatives from other countries!"

I dared one little sigh of relief. "So then I'll be one of quite a few speakers, meaning, I take it, that each one of us will be allowed a very few minutes?"

Jeanette must have felt that I was about to accept this still incredible assignment. "Yes, this is an important point," she said. "Each speaker will have about five minutes," she replied somewhat gravely. "But not you, Marlene. We have given this quite some thought, you know. We know what we are asking. This is why I call you now as the president of the group, and the program chairman will call you later for the details. We thought that I should try to win you to be the main speaker of the evening. We ask you to take no less than thirty minutes. We are sure that you understand our motivation, and we also know that for the same reason you will oblige."

"Of course," I said, "God being my helper." I replaced the receiver. It was midnight.

Christmas came and went; my thoughts concentrated on the forthcoming task. Over and over I called to mind that this was war, this was 1943, and by lawful definition I was an enemy alien. I was to be the main speaker on a program of international scope: I was to represent the enemy country to a group of church people whose sons served their country under fire.

But stronger than all of that I sensed that one love that motivated my new friends to plan and prepare as they did. And the desire grew within me to serve them in the same vein of divine love, and to the best of my ability.

Those are the wonderful occasions when the conversations with the Unseen One bring the most real response. I submitted my thinking to his love, and word by word amassed what I should say that would honor fact over fiction, clearness over disguise, candor over concealment. But above all, good would overcome evil, and the Lord Christ would come out on top. And I began to feel the first bit of relief from what until then had seemed a very tall order.

The day we gathered in the parish hall, the Christmas decorations were still up, looking fresh and well cared for. As I entered, I could sense the good spirit that had brought these people together. It floated in the air; it was in the humming of their voices.

In a special room, I greeted the other participants in the program. I shook hands all around, and not without trepidation. Jeanette, the president, and Irene, the program chairman, made us comfortable.

The moment came when, with a special air of dignity, Irene escorted the other five speakers to the head table. Ilona, in her attractive Hungarian costume, stood out. The lights were dimmed; the room was candlelit.

"All right, Marlene," Madame President said, and took us to the center places waiting for us.

My "enemy alien" heart beat fast and furious. On our way, I noticed many friendly faces beautified by the warm light of the candles. I noted the Christmas greens, the lovely fresh flowers, the colorful ornaments. The head table was arranged against a background of the flags of many nations, multicolored, like the specter of the sun.

The people stood behind their chairs quietly, captivated no less, I am sure, than myself by the mysterious beauty, the air of love about us.

Then, as Jeanette showed me to my place next to hers, with all eyes upon us, I noticed the special place cards on the head table. I saw mine.

Like the drowning man who sees a flashback of his life in the fraction of a second, I saw my place card and I recapitulated once again, but now as if by force: This is (now) 1944, America at war with Germany, our minds bared to the forces of destruction. The sons of these people are in the armed forces and under fire. It is Christmas, and I, Miss Enemy Alien, am about to represent the enemy country to this group.

I could neither breathe nor swallow as I seized the back of my chair, staring at my place card. In a marshmallow for a basis, three tiny flags had been arranged. The church flag was to the left, the flag of the United States to the right. But in the center, there was the flag under which I had been born and grown up, not the swastika, but the colors black, white, and red of the Germany of my commitment that I had loved as I should but that had been brought to naught by its own failures.

I was totally unprepared for such display of understanding and of generous love. I confess that I have never again been touched by a comparably profound emotion. I lowered my head deeply before God and these, his people, who knew and enacted his love, present with us in the Child of Bethlehem. After some moments of silence over that hall, Jeanette's voice got through to me. Her eyes were shining with warmth and love as she opened the meeting. She addressed herself to the festive crowd as she said that they were well aware of doing something quite extraordinary. Then she turned to me, for another surprise for which I was equally unprepared. She said, "And now we ask Mrs. Maertens to say grace for us."

I surrendered to God; I fought for the control of my voice. None of the many prayers to be offered before a meal came to mind. What did come to my mind was quite simple, and with my heart ringing with his love, I proclaimed it as our Thanksgiving:

For unto us is born this day in the city of David a Savior, which is Christ the Lord—and of his love, there is no end.

We sat down to our festive meal and the International Night. To me, it no longer mattered what I would say later on. All would be right. For God was with us. He was at the head table and in the crowd. His was the glory, but we held, in wide-open arms, the peace on earth that passes all understanding. It kept our hearts and minds. Good will toward men, it was right here.

3

EPIPHANY

The shepherds in the Judean field were not the Child's only visitors. They were the first, to be sure, and when they had left they began to tell of their experiences to whomever they met. They praised God as they spread what they had heard and seen.

Shortly afterward another group came. They were strangers to these parts. Three Wise Men from the east, the Bible calls them. Some people think of them as kings, others as magi. They were men of status, and they brought precious gifts from their lands far away from Judea. By all comparable standards, they were very different from those humble shepherds; they were even Gentiles, while the shepherds were Jews. It must not be forgotten that it was the Jews to whom God had promised his Messiah, the Christ. But all the differences together cannot measure up to the importance of what they suddenly had in common: both groups heard God's call to go to Bethlehem, to see, and to worship; and both obeyed without questioning. They went, they saw, they worshiped, and they came away believing, the shepherds and the kings. By this we, of God's Today, know that from the beginning God revealed himself to the poor and the rich, the lowly and those of high estate, the simple and the high-minded, the Jew and the Gentile—to all mankind.

The church commemorates the visit of the Magi to the Child in Bethlehem and the significance of this visit as the Epiphany, or the Manifestation of Christ to the Gentiles.

Matthew tells the story upon which the Epiphany season rests. It is truly another story in God's Today. Herod, king in Jerusalem, receives in audience those three Wise Men from the east. They have an urgent but highly embarrassing question to ask. "Where is he that is born King of the Jews?"

Herod doubts that he is hearing correctly. He is the king, appointed by Rome. He gropes for an answer; he hides his bewilderment. Is there something he should know but does not know? Who could have been born to rob him of his throne? He is deeply troubled and his worries increase as his august visitors speak of a star in the sky, that it was this star which had led them this far. They had to find that king. "Where is he?" they insisted. "We have come all this way, we shall go on till we find him; yes, we want to worship him!"

At such display of persistence, King Herod got truly alarmed and the establishment with him. He would want to seek counsel immediately. He put his visitors off; he would let them know the answer very soon.

Tormenting thoughts. This was no nonsense. Could it have to do with God's promise of old to send his Messiah? Was he about to come to liberate the Jews? That possibility held no comfort for King Herod. He was the king, he sat on the throne; whatever power Rome had meted out to him—he held it.

Yet he called together all the chief priests and the scribes of the people, learned men all and trusted guardians of the faith, and he bade them tell him where this Christ should be born.

The answer was easily available: the prophet was quoted:

"And thou, Bethlehem, in the land of Juda, art not the least among the princes of Juda: for out of thee shall come a Governor, that shall rule my people Israel."

Herod's reaction was swift. Never mind the prophet, never mind God's promise. He intended to keep his throne. His thoughts took shape. Enough of this commotion; he would know how to dispose of this threat diligently. Of course, it had to be kept a top secret. And as to the foreigners, he would simply use them to set his plan in motion.

He called them back, maintaining strict secrecy. He made them feel welcome, engaged with them in good conversation. Yes, he had good news for them. If not entirely perfect, then at least helpful. But first he wanted to check with them what they had told him about that star. He should like to know more about it. When did it appear, and then what happened? And as they readily replied, King Herod recognized with renewed horror the definite connection with some of the things he had learned, even with the prophecy concerning his city of Bethlehem.

He knew how to control himself; and outwardly jovial, he disclosed his good news: they should look for the child in Bethlehem. "Go and find him," he urged them on, "and on your way back come and tell me where he is. For I too would like to worship him."

At that, the travelers hurried on. Presently, up in the sky there was their star again that had led them from the east. Great was their joy. This was God's action. Their reaction was faithfully to accept and to follow. Thus they were led to the Child. They beheld him in his mother's arms, in his humble surroundings. To them, it was a scene of peace and utter loveliness; they fell down upon their knees and worshiped the Child. Then they opened up the treasures they had brought and joyfully presented the precious gifts. It is good to imagine what they thought and how they felt.

And now the long journey home. Which road to take. Of course they should stop at Jerusalem, in deference to King Herod's wishes. The Bible story does not tell us that they doubted him. The Bible says that it was God who warned them not to return to King Herod, and following God they quietly "departed into their own country another way." In their very persons they took with them their new knowledge that they had accepted in faith. They carried it beyond the borders of the land of the Children of Israel, into the realm of the Gentiles, into the wide world.

The Manifestation of Christ to the Gentiles does not end, is not complete with the Three Wise Men arriving home filled with their new knowledge two thousand historic years ago. It is another timeless story pertaining to God's Today, for us to know, to grasp, and to apply to our own life. For now God uses men, acts through them. Manifestation and Making-Known have blended as much as the word "Gentile" no longer means heathen or pagan but blends the heathen with the Christian-in-name-only. The story I shall tell later in this chapter was selected to exemplify just this.

Before we get to that, I should like to offer the account of my own definition of my own Epiphany. Some readers might find it helpful by comparison; others might reject it as strictly untheological. To me, this my thesis is logical as well as dear, and cause for much gratitude as the span of life lengthens.

There has been ample reason in my life to contemplate the following question in its two aspects: How was Christ made manifest to me? And, How did I make him known to others? Is it not that in life temporal all things pertaining to life eternal must be cemented by solid knowledge lest they float off into the realm of an empty emotionalism or, worse, into superstition of what it is all about? To me, there is no doubt that neither my baptism at the age of three weeks, nor my confirmation fifteen years later, gave me, alongside with communicant church membership, more than the basic authenticity of my faith.

Yet somehow I have known, as long as I can remember, the love for the Babe in the manger. But it took a considerable step into adolescence, if not maturity, until I knew that even this love was not my own resolve: it was God's gift to me. Just the same, this live love, exciting, happy, curious-for-more, was with me when I was enrolled in school, a youngster not quite six years old. From the beginning of this schooling, our schedules included two lessons each week called "Religion." They were continued for ten full years at the same rate; then the church took over for one year's instructions prior to the great day of confirmation. This was a very special day indeed, held in the middle of the week; and on the Sunday before, in the main service, there would be a thorough examination of the entire class in the presence of the congregation.

Ten years of "Religion" in school twice a week meant a step by step growing into the given facts of our faith, yet as one special subject among the others of a general educational curriculum. The lessons were of course gauged to the capacity of the growing, the expanding mind. At first, there were just stories told, from the New and from the Old Testament. They were convincingly told to the extent that all those people became truly alive, graphically alive and familiar like people we know today. Yet as far as stories about Jesus were concerned, it was different from the beginning. They stood out, he was their center, the focal point and towering culmination. All other stories depicted important events with important people who were with (or without) God; his stories depicted Jesus. Today I know that we come to know God because we have come to know Jesus.

Back to the school years. As time went on, our lessons

had more ambitious names. There was "Biblical History," there was "History of the Bible." There was "Old Testament" and there was "New Testament" in a year's curriculum. Our studies included Luther's Small Catechism; yet they were not doctrinal in character. Memory speaks up now and bids me tell that we memorized a great deal. It began with the Ten Commandments and the Lord's Prayer; it included quite a number of psalms and, of course, long, very long, German hymns.

To dogma and doctrine we were introduced in confirmation class. I became aware of the facts of my own faith. I realized the truth of my own love of God no less than his love for me. How could this be? In God's love came my answer: God the Holy Spirit.

God the Holy Spirit: It was not difficult to deal with, to ponder, and to accept. It meant the sudden disclosure of the treasure I was holding all along. It provided the simple explanation of myself, my place in the world. By God's own will I became his creature; by his Son's love and sacrifice (and my faith in him) I was redeemed from all sin in this world, and by his Holy Spirit dwelling within me I am granted to know and to say this. By his grace, I can say it now.

This may be the explanation of the fact that I have come to look upon those blessed years of "Religion in School" as upon my own Epiphany, my personal Having-Christ-Made-Manifest to me. Today, I know to thank God for diligent teachers; for the many and simple ways in which the Lord Christ can be, and is being, made manifest to Jew and Gentile alike. As it was then, so long ago, so it is now, transcended in meaning, a vital part of our activity in God's everlasting Today.

For to know the Lord Christ is never an end in itself, no treasure to be kept in the vaults of a bank. It is an ever-new beginning, a daily new obligation—not to preach to man what he preached, but "to preach" him. To witness to him. To make him manifest. The shepherds proclaimed the glad tidings; so did the Magi. And we must proclaim the Lord Christ manifest in the thick of our world Today.

The thick of our world today: from the mere meaning of the word "problem," our world today is not really different from yesteryear, or from the time when the Magi came to ask their all-important question of King Herod of Judea. We have to return to him for a moment for the purpose of a relevant introduction of the story which is to follow.

We remember that King Herod had been appointed by Rome. We know that he had ruled his land for a number of years when he received those strange visitors. It is their question that survives: "Where is he that is born King of the Jews? We have seen his star in the east and are come to worship him."

The man whom history came to call King Herod the Great felt his throne tremble. "All Jerusalem" with him was profoundly shocked, meaning all those who sat secure in the establishment under his rule. And here is the revealing twist: threatened in his secular power, as Herod believes himself to be, he takes counsel with those who are in power with him, the chief priests and the scribes. But he has no dynastic problem to proffer for their solution; he poignantly demands to be brought up to date on the existing prophecies of old, the prophecies of the men of God. No, not all of it: all he wants to know is "where the Christ should be born." They corroborate his fears: the place is Bethlehem, just a few miles to the south, and in his realm.

Herod takes it from there. With deceit for the foreigners, he makes his decision: all male infants in Bethlehem are to be killed. There we are: the secular power against the rule of the Eternal. The human thought—I know how to deal with this!—above the divine word and its definite claim to supremacy. Transferred to the human level: here is the deceptive, the diplomatic falsehood versus the trust of the believer. God speaks, God acts, but man reacts with his own thoughts. They do not ignore God. Quite the contrary: they outwit God. It is man against God. And here, in our story of old yet relevant today, man seeks to outwit God even at the dawn of his own redemption.

No, the picture has not changed much. We still do not rally around God the Christ, the Lord of all things. We do not live him. We neither live him inside nor outside of our churches. We do not take our directions from him and boldly apply them to each and every problem of our Today. We do not make him quietly manifest, unerringly so, to the world in which we live. But then: What else was Martin Luther King's life but one flaming manifestation of Christ and his love to all people and the profound entreaty to take life from there, and only from there?

I pray that the story that follows now shall do its part to underscore the issue and to bring into focus both the dilemma and its solution. The story could have happened anywhere in the world, and in its gist it has. It can easily happen in our own country and at certain times and events it seemed as if we were quite close to it, to its intellectual content. To me, it has happened in my native country, Germany.

It was the time when National Socialism ruled the country with an iron hand, with power supreme, suffering indeed "none other gods but me." But while the Lord God in his First Commandment still places man before the choice of accepting or rejecting, Adolf Hitler's ideology allowed no room for such freedom. He who did not fit the pattern, he who still thought he could object, was "out," especially if his objection was grounded in his faith in God. At first it was still cleverly disguised, but it soon came out in the open: the holders of the temporal power considered themselves also the holders of the eternal power. The Author of the Eternal Power was incompatible. They were very right. They spoke by the pressure of imposed legislation—and we know how God speaks. It really was incompatible!

But to reject National Socialism did not mean one's retirement to some peaceful place where one could mind one's own business. To be out meant persecution, concentration camp, loss of human dignity; it meant an agonized death.

With faith in itself and utter conviction, National Socialism began building the "Thousand Year Reich," as they called it. The foundation upon which it was being erected was "blood and soil." It meant that the pure Germanic blood of its constituents would be prerequisite as its stream of life, while the sacred German soil would be the ground of its constancy. A great number of very special bricks went into the structure, and from among those I shall pick but three to illustrate the story I have begun to tell.

It was the fateful year 1935, late in the spring, and several months before the diabolical "Nuremberg Laws" were enacted. These, by the way, were to become not mere bricks, they were pillars in the structure of the Thousand Year Reich. Their spirit was already in evidence.

At this time, my husband and I were living in the north of Germany. He held the post of a Commanding Officer of a large naval institution. He had been a professional sailor for twenty-five years, sworn to loyalty first to Germany's last emperor, Kaiser Wilhelm II, then to the Weimar Republic, and now to the person of Adolf Hitler. While it would have been possible to seek release from the oath under the previous government, it was not permissible now, as long as a man was of "Aryan blood and believed in Germany." And, as many men of unquestionable integrity tried for an honorable attitude in a dishonorable situation, so did he.

As his wife, I had my share in his prominent position which meant a life in the proverbial goldfish bowl. It was not easy, for I had much to hide. My active membership in the "outlawed" Confessing Church was to me the most important thing, and I remember my clear stand with gratitude to God and with joy. The Confessing Church consisted of clergy and laymen who opposed National Socialism as incompatible to the Christian faith and its claim on human conduct. Many of them paid for their stand with their lives.

But an even blacker mark against me, in the eyes of the ruling ideology, was the fact that I knew myself not to be of the required pure Aryan blood. To be German born, the Christian daughter of Christian parents, was not good enough. I used the term "I knew myself to be" a moment ago with descriptive care: for my disqualification from being counted a true German was not publicly known.

My lot for the moment was therefore to go on living with God, but in constant fear of discovery. If I speak of fear, I do not think so much of myself. I think of my husband: under the new ideology, I did not qualify to be his wife. I had not sworn an oath to loyalty to Adolf Hitler, but I too had a vow to think of. It was freely given to God, at the altar of my church, to be my husband's helpmate, for better for worse, until death . . .

With all the skill in our reach, we cautiously guarded my secret. Its disclosure would have meant certain death, not just for me, but for my husband and for many we held dear.

Outwardly unmoved, we attended to our daily duties. I tried earnestly to permeate them pronouncedly with the love of God and love of the neighbor. It is against this background that we shall now inspect the three bricks I am borrowing from the construction of the Thousand Year Reich for the illustration of our story.

The first represented existence itself, human beings, meaning Germany's future in her children. The Führer needed more than he had. The Führer would need more soldiers. That had to be kept in mind. And so the making of children was publicly promoted. A child was no longer God's blessing to married love. A child was to be made for Germany, for the Führer. Married or not, the status of the parents did not matter. The child mattered. Preferably it should be blond and blue-eyed, a specimen of the master race. It had to be German. I recall one speech Adolf Hitler made before a vast assembly of the party's Women's Association. The most wonderful contribution the German woman could make to the Reich was accomplished the moment she gave birth to a well-shaped, sound new German, he said. The audience shrieked in enchanted approval.

Another incidence to illustrate the situation. One morning the young wife of an officer on my husband's staff came to see me. They were a fine couple, both offspring of old families, both very blond and blue-eyed. Beyond that, both were God-fearing, devout Christians, and parents of two infant children. Believing that she could trust as well as confide in me, she told me of the visit of a young man in party uniform the day before. Standing at her door, he asked to come in as if on official business, and she had not the right to refuse him. Matter-of-factly he stated his case. The party had selected her and her husband to suggest to them the production of another child. They stood highly in favor; they were the perfect example of what the Führer wanted his Germans to look like. His generosity was great: the child would not be a financial hardship on them. After his infancy, he would be taken over by the state and properly educated for his future role as the German elite. To them, the parents, not only would fall high honor but also considerable financial advantages on the tax level. My friend, whose husband was away on a cruise, trembled with rage as she told the story. You see, she could not throw the man out. You could not throw the State out. If you did, the State threw you out.

The State claimed, and held, the absolute power over each person in the realm, regardless of his status or station in life. Step by giant step, without any allowances of compromises, National Socialism blotted out, then superseded all former statutes and values. Christianity was soon singled out as the very threat to the successful furtherance of the ideology, it was recognized as the believer's stronghold. Therefore it had to be fought. It's their souls we want. And if Christianity could not be run over right away, at least it had to be coordinated to the blueprint of the State.

Sadly, this is not the place to talk of the church of Christ asserting her mission. This is the place to look at brick number two as it points to some of the things National Socialism did in its initial fight against Christianity. It did not actually come out in the open: "The Almighty" and "Providence" were on Adolf Hitler's lips. But more and more I heard it said by people on that famous middle road, "Really, I do believe in God, but as to that carpenter of Nazareth . . . now you must admit that we can do without him." Yet the New Testament remained around (with proper misgivings as to Paul, that converted Jew), while the Old Testament was more and more classified as unsuitable for upright Germans. Who cared about those old Jews anyway? On the other hand, that whole book was yet suitable as a good account of their base character, their low morals, their schemings and fraudulences, and of God's punishment. And as it turned out not to be so easy "to do without the Carpenter of Nazareth," he was more and more made over, he was not a Jew but an Aryan. He was actually a hero. He preached heroic things. So he got himself cruci-

fied, and by whom? You guessed it. It justified all the more
that we'd finally deal with them. How did it go? "An eye
for an eye, and a tooth for a tooth." And with righteous
indignation the official hate of the Jews served the noble
effort to purge and to cleanse the Christian faith and to
make it palatable for the True German.

Accordingly, alongside of many innovations in the life
of the church, the clergy were told what to preach and
what not. Hymns, as well as Scripture lessons, were to be
selected with the positive minimum of reference to the
origin of our faith. There was even one try at "aryanizing"
the Lord's Prayer. All in all, in the final analysis it might
not be too difficult to doctor the Christian faith to fit Germany's shield, and Adolf Hitler would be the Savior who
carried this shield against the foe. His picture was already
found on the altar of some churches—of some, I should
like to underscore.

The third brick emerges now more and more clearly.
It represents the application of National Socialism upon the
shaping of the human mind; we call it brainwashing today.
There was a slogan effectively used in those days more than
thirty years ago but by no means out of print today. This
slogan is a nutshell version of National Socialist ideology,
a religion, like all man-made ideologies, to those who believe in them. Here is what may be called the Nazi creed:

> I Believe in Myself
> I Believe in My People
> I Believe in My Sword!

It is good to read it over several times to let it soak in. It
is good to pause long enough to recite the Apostles' Creed
and face that choice clearly that we, under National Socialism, were denied. It is good to pause long enough to give
thanks for the freedom of the choice. But most of all it
would be good to pause long enough and take careful in-
ventory on that question: How much am I, is my country,

subject to this, I Believe in Myself, I Believe in My People, I Believe in My Sword?

We cannot become casual about the ongoing deification of self. Grateful indeed for the free choice, I think of Joshua. "Choose you this day whom ye will serve . . . but as for me and my house, we will serve the Lord."

There you have the three bricks that helped to build the Thousand Year Reich: more select children for Germany; fight against everything un-German, especially the Christian faith; fighting for and securing (for the next thousand years) the German creed of faith in self, faith in the own people, faith in the sword.

There was a family in our midst: father, mother, three teen-age children, likable people, a joy to know. Blond and blue-eyed all, their enthusiasm for the new precept and its author was, if not catching, at least acknowledgeable for its undisguised sincerity. They were totally sold, so much so that one day Mrs. Miller, as we shall call her, came to me to announce happily that she and her husband had decided to give a child to the Führer. "How very nice to know that you are expecting again after so many years," I said uneasily, thanking her for her confidence. She laughed out heartily: "Oh no, Carl and I have merely decided to start one. You know the Führer needs them!" It was as simple as that. It would be a son. For the Führer. The Creator, the Lord over all things, needed not to be bothered.

Just the same, God did say "Yes," and before one year was up the happy parents welcomed a sound ten-pound son, their third. The mother's confinement was brief; she came to see me again when the baby was not yet two weeks old. She had something important to discuss with me and it was obvious that she expected to please me. I never doubted the sincerity of her affection for me, and, under the circumstances, I had to be grateful that she did not know that she wasted it on an ethnic outcast.

With warmth and emotion she told me of their decision

to have the baby baptized after all, instead of the German rite of Name-giving, now the new fashion. She smiled. "We really have you in mind in connection with our decision, you are so wonderfully old-fashioned!"

I could not refuse this unusual compliment on the ground that no child could ever be baptized "with me in mind." But alas, this was not the time to speak of the Sacrament of Baptism. Instead, and oh, how deeply burns the guilt of silence, I nodded pleasantly and promised to arrange for our attendance.

This was not all. The crux of the matter was about to come. "There is just one more thing I would like to ask of you," Mrs. Miller said. "You are such good friends with Chaplain Schallehn, and we would appreciate it if you could convey our request to him. We know he will preach a fine sermon that day, but we should like to let him know our choice of a text. Would you please tell him to preach on this true expression of our faith, of our hope for strength as we know it now?"

My heart stood still in sudden anguish. I was not privileged to tell her in just so many simple words that the true expression of her faith, I believe in myself, I believe in my people, I believe in my sword, was totally unchristian and therefore unadmissible to a Christian rite. But how could I refuse to pass on this request and not become publicly guilty of being un-German? Why did I not simply say that a sermon should always be based upon a word of God, not of man? And, similar to King Herod, I thought one thing but said another.

"No, my dear," and it came pleasantly enough, "I beg to disagree. The preparation of a baptism should remain the prerogative of parents and minister. I am sure Pastor Schallehn will gladly discuss everything with you."

A few days later, the chaplain's visit was announced. As he stood in the door to my sitting room, his arm raised in the obligatory Hitler salute, I knew what brought him. He

was tense and nervous; there was no sign of his usual
pleasant self.

As if I did not know! I asked him in; we sat down after
I had carefully covered the telephone and all outlets. I tried
to make the beginning easy for him, for these were not
the days of an exchange of confidences. "She has asked
you," I whispered.

"You know I cannot do this," he blurted out. "I would
fail God, fail my office." And as if in shock, he enumerated
the consequences of a refusal.

I knew indeed. His existence was at stake, perhaps even
his life. He had a young wife, a newborn child (a gift from
God). They were a family born to be Germans. But above
all else, he had committed his life to the service of God.
He saw the decisive choice he had to make. Would he cast
aside the Lord Christ, the Way, the Truth, and the Life?

Yes, Pastor Schallehn was placed before a clear choice:
Ideology versus Religion. Which road would he take? Here
was one of those moments which have taught me to comprehend more and more clearly, even more and more
simply, God's voice and God's hand in our life. The event,
that which happens to us, is not the important thing. Important is what we, on God's hand, make of it.

I do not recall the detail of Pastor Schallehn's and my
conversation on that day. We talked on quietly for quite
some time. But this I do remember with an unforgettable
certainty: The peace that passes understanding, the peace
that the world cannot give, had been made manifest in us.
We shared it, as Pastor Schallehn left, newly strengthened.

On the appointed day, a happy and festive group gathered
in the Millers' living room. A little altar had been prepared
in one corner, graced by a small cross which was flanked by
flowers and candles. It was hung with the German flag. I
can still feel the apprehension of my heart as the ceremony
began.

Pastor Schallehn entered the room, followed by the radiant parents with their baby son. The man in his clerical robe, the Bible in his left palm and covered by his right hand, never looked more meaningful to me. His face was calm, if not serene. He took his place before the altar, then faced the happy parents. Mrs. Miller cradled her baby in her arms.

It was a lovely scene to behold. It was just underneath, and behind it, that things were so terribly wrong. For a fleeting moment I caught myself yearning for a justification: Why should he not be placed under the motto "I believe in myself, I believe in my people, I believe in my sword"? It radiated such good things: strength, independency, dependency on oneself, faith in familiar helpers . . .

Pastor Schallehn's voice cut right into those thoughts. The sermon came first. Calmly he began: "The word of Holy Scripture upon which this child will be baptized is found in The Book of Isaiah, chapter 40, verse 31:

> "But they that wait upon the Lord shall renew their strength; they shall mount up with wings as eagles; they shall run, and not be weary; and they shall walk, and not faint."

To this day, I recall the sensation of fear like an ice-cold grip around my heart. To this day, I am grateful to God that he has still spared so many of us from truly understanding the full extent of Pastor Schallehn's courage in faith. To this day I wish nothing more fervently than that we should all learn from our experiences and put them to good use.

What Pastor Schallehn had done sounded so simple, but was so much. He had matched the "spiritual hopes" of these parents for a good, strong life for their son. He had reached to the only source that can nourish such hopes, and in doing so, he had offended the faith of the land. He had added grave insult to grave injury by selecting a text from the Jewish Old Testament for a German child.

Pastor Schallehn was rewarded: he got away with it—this time. He had indeed made God in Christ manifest to the Gentiles!

We have remained friends to this day. I reminded him of this story several years ago when, as an aging minister, he felt frustrated about the apathy of the youth entrusted to his care, young people of confirmation age. As we talked, the circle of our concern widened. The picture emerged clearly. The wise men are still asking the secular power: "Where is he that is born King of the Jews? For we have seen his star, and are come to worship him."

4

LENT

The word "Lent" derives from an old Anglo-Saxon word meaning "spring." When winter has run its course, when nature is about to reawaken and spring is at hand, if not here, the church gets ready for its season dedicated to penitence, to the mourning of sins. It is in part based upon the recollection of our Lord's forty days in the wilderness, his fasting, his suffering, the temptations taken upon himself for our sake. It concentrates on just that; at its end looms the cross toward which we walk with him and we are not wont to look beyond that.

But thoughts of Lent as a season of the church year seem to present a friendly temptation, to dwell at length on the many ways, the various forms in which it is being observed by the congregations of God all through the country. The schools of thought on the subject and their expression, the rules including guidelines for personal behavior, have shaped these annual observances toward stepping up of congregational activity both in church and parish house. Interdenominational noonday services, more often than not sponsored by local church councils, are a very real benefit especially to the working community. They round off a special season with special events. All in all, it is a highly active period of six weeks and to the living, there is joy in activity.

I do not purport to be critical of our existing customs, nor do I consider our observation of Lent from Ash Wednesday to Good Friday with any question mark on my mind. In the contrary, I like it very much. But I should like to state my own view of the general activity: No other event in the Christian year, no evaluation of the Christian's Today, calls us more earnestly, more strongly, to an examination of our own self. The question as I see it: What does the Lord Christ really mean to me, and where do I really stand in my discipleship?

To answer these questions with validity, I first have to take a deep breath. This deep breath will signify that I am a living part of the Creation. It will also signify that I am willing to make clear to myself just Who I Am in God's Creation.

With fear and with love I must confess to the Eternal God that I am his creature, allowed by him to be in his world. I am a definite part of his Today; I am fallen into sin. And I am a sinner.

I know that in his love God has redeemed even me. He has done that by the supreme sacrifice of his Son, Jesus Christ, Godhead on earth. Without faith in Jesus Christ, I am nothing. With it, I am one in him. With it, and only with it, may I stretch out my hand to my companions on the road on which he walks, on which he leads. I have to see that clearly. I have to see him clearly.

He went into the wilderness and for our sake fasted forty days and forty nights. He subdued the flesh to the spirit; he was tortured in both. He came face to face with hunger, with frustration, with idolatry. He was severely challenged to prove his power as the Son of God. He did not falter, he pointed to God. He did not complain at being tempted, he chased the tempter away. "Get thee hence, Satan: for it is written, Thou shalt worship the Lord thy God, and him only shalt thou serve."

He withstood the temptation for us who succumb. Free of sin, he gathers us unto him on his road. His road leads up to Jerusalem, to a triumphant entry with cheering crowds, to the nightmare of betrayal and interrogation and "third degree" at the hands of those who by their very attitude reneged their high office as the guardians of God's law, on to his certain, ignoble death.

He knew it all, of course, and he spoke to his disciples about it, now saying it for the last time: "We go up to Jerusalem, and all things that are written by the prophets concerning the Son of Man shall be accomplished." Again, as before, they did not understand it, but they understood him and they had faith. They did not leave him. They walked up to Jerusalem with him.

This pilgrimage to Jerusalem, Jesus of Nazareth's final walk through life temporal to its agonizing ending, is commemorated by his church in the setting of the Lenten season.

The pilgrimage up to Jerusalem, led by him who had fasted in the wilderness, suffered the tortures of temptation for the utter identification of Self in body and soul, in his timeless service to all mankind, this too is our Today.

There is a story in the Bible of special meaning to me in my own search for identification with my Lord Christ in Lent. Much as I enjoy, as already stated, the stepped-up activities, the additional services, the parish dinners, the special preachers and speakers to relevant subjects, there is yet a yearning within me for "More." I can define this "More." Above all else, it is authentic; I would not dare to ignore or deny it. It suggests the desire to find the simplest possible expression of the impact of Lent upon me. Finally, this inner call for "More" challenges me to find some resolve which remains both valid and applicable to my day-by-day living through all of God's Today.

I have called that story "Jesus Only," for that, to me, is

its message and its application. Matthew, Mark, and Luke tell it. The church calls it "The Transfiguration of Christ" and observes it for its theological content on a special feast day in August.

Jesus takes three of his disciples for a walk. They walk away, away from the others, from people, from things. He may want to let them share the blessing of solitude which he himself seeks from time to time. Whatever the purpose: they walk, walk on till they get to the foot of a mountain, and they climb it. Up there, "closer to heaven" as we might want to say, Jesus begins to pray. Tired from the walk and ready for some sleep, they watch him. They see him as they have never seen him before. He looks quite different; he looks changed, transfigured. His face shines like the sun, his garment glistens whiter than snow. They gaze and gaze, and behold, he is no longer alone. As if in a daze now, they see him in the company of two men, long glorified in God's keeping, yet utterly familiar to their thoughts. They are Moses and Elias, and they are talking with their Lord. Above them, a white cloud is approaching as if moved by an invisible hand.

They can hear what Moses and Elias are saying to their Master. It sounds familiar. The time to fulfill his mission on earth, in Jerusalem, was at hand. Of course they had heard him speak of it before. They had inwardly retained but never really understood it. Now they heard it again, and in this company!

They saw and they heard: the reality of the moment consisted of apparition and vision, of vigilance and sleep, and of the white cloud slowly approaching. They enjoyed it all. "It is good for us to be here," says Peter and he suggests to the Lord, "Let us make here three tabernacles; one for thee, and one for Moses, and one for Elias!"

Just then the white cloud envelops them completely and to their utter terror. They fall down upon their faces; they hear a Voice saying, "This is my beloved Son: hear him."

Silence; it is quiet as the cloud lifts up. Jesus touches them and says, "Rise, and have no fear." The three disciples rally. They look about them. They see *Jesus Only*.

This "Jesus Only" has become my personal identification with Lent, with walking up to Jerusalem with him through those forty days. It is an experience that gains in momentum as the years go by. In wanting, in striving, in struggling to see "Jesus Only," one slowly advances to the reality of "In him we live, and move, and have our being" in its full impact upon our life Today. Also, as the white cloud lifts, to see "Jesus Only" then equates to see *all* there really is to be seen in this world.

This "Jesus Only" is also the heading of the extraordinary story I have selected to tell in the context of this chapter, Lent. It is the story of a still young woman, now at the peak of her life. She is a doctor of medicine, a Roman Catholic, a nun of the Medical Mission Sisters, and all these qualifications blend into one expression of discipleship of her Lord Jesus Christ.

To me, she is a friend in Christ Jesus, and in my heart I call her my child. I met her first in 1941, shortly after her thirteenth birthday. A few months earlier she had been restored to her parents, Hitler refugees from Vienna together with great numbers of other Jews, who tried to make a new life for themselves in New York. Before it became possible for them to leave Vienna, their daughter and only child had been taken to safety in England with a transport of 150 Jewish children who were to be placed with English families and homes. At the cruel and bitter parting, our little family did not know if they would ever see each other again.

Even though I am related to the family through my mother, we had no connection with each other. We had never met; I had but the barest knowledge of their existence. They lived in another country and they were not of our faith. That was sufficient to have a natural barrier between people under what was called normal living conditions. God took care of all this (unintended) nonsense. According to his will, we met in New York. I came face to face with their intense suffering. They were totally uprooted, without possessions, and had to leave behind many members of their immediate families to the certainty of concentration camp and indeed death. Both going on fifty, they now had to struggle for a new existence. But obviously nothing tormented them more than to be separated from their only child. At that time there was but a dim hope of getting her across the Atlantic Ocean to American safety and to their loving arms.

The merciful God let it happen. One day, a few months before I met the child, I received a postcard from her mother. The text is engraved in my heart. "Formerly I could not sleep," it said, "for longing to see that blond little head once again on the pillow beside mine, and now I cannot sleep because I do!"

I saw the three of them together when I went up to New York from Kentucky where I lived at that time. I had to attend to matters of foremost importance to me. They required my undivided attention, for my very existence in this country, where I had no home rights yet, was involved. Under recently issued government regulations I could leave the country for the purpose of applying for an immigration visa to the United States at the Consulate General in Havana, Cuba. In those days one could go there intentionally and directly. My status in the United States was untenable. As an admitted guest I could not do paid work; in other words, I could not earn my living.

It was then that I saw little Hanna for the first time, about one year after I had met her parents. She seized my outstretched hand as if she greeted an old friend. There was an unusual quality to her joy; I detected it without being able to grasp it. However, she made it quite clear that she would very much like to have a heart-to-heart talk with me.

With all those preparations for my trip to Cuba, the many errands to comply with all legal requirements foremost on my mind, I was rather reluctant. But she remained joyfully adamant and she came to see me alone at my hotel room.

"I have been anxious to meet you and to tell you something," she began, her voice barely above a whisper, her eyes sparkling. "I know you are a Christian," she continued, "and I want you to know that I am a Christian too!"

"Hanna, I don't believe that you know what you are saying!" I cried. "This is a very big thing to say for a little girl of thirteen and in your situation. Have you spoken to your parents about this?"

Her eyes darkened. "You know that I cannot do that; they would not understand, and"—almost tenderly—"I know that they cannot understand this. But you must help me." We both fell silent.

I did not know what to think. Here before me was this youngster, apparently oblivious to her most recent past, her escape from Vienna, the separation from her parents, and their miraculous reunion in a new country. What mattered to her more than anything else was to tell me that she was a Christian. Suddenly I had the whole picture before my mind's eye. I saw her parents, honorable people and members of the Jewish faith, broken in spirit, victims with countless others of man's inhumanity to man. I could imagine the insufferable load of hate, injustice, evil, they were forced to bear. How could they possibly find a shortcut through their present outlook, that to them every non-Jew was a Nazi, every Nazi a German, and (would it were true!) every German a Christian. No, there was no hope, this was not the time to penetrate to reason and truth.

"Hanna," I said, now in turmoil, "you are still very young, too young to deal with a problem of such magni-

tude. Let's wait a few years, we can always talk about it—"
She interrupted me with determination. "There is no problem for me, Tante Marlene. I have found the Lord Jesus,
and I shall never let go of him again." It shone from her
eyes.

I took a deep breath while she watched me eagerly. This
was real. Here were two together in his name.

I took her hand in mine and asked: "How did it happen that you found the Lord Jesus—or that the Lord
Jesus found you? Had it to do with the family to whom
you were entrusted in England? Was it their good influence?"

Her smile was loving and sweet. "If anything might have
kept me away, it was my dear foster-parents," she said.
"Uncle Fred was Church of England and Aunt Marjorie
was Christian Scientist and they never could agree."

I listened with bated breath. Was this really a thirteen-
year-old child? She went on, with radiant eyes above a
whispering voice.

"They were extremely kind to me, and I love them very
much. They trusted me enough to let me ride the train
up to London and to look around by myself. It was the
time of the blitz, you know. One day, I was just visiting St.
Paul's Cathedral."

"Were you impressed by what you saw there?" I asked,
thinking of the twelve-year-old Jewish refugee girl from
Vienna all by herself in one of Christendom's foremost
shrines.

She nodded pleasantly but brushed the question aside.
It was not relevant. She pursued the point.

"There were a great many people in St. Paul's when the
sirens were sounded. With them I went to the air raid
shelter nearby. The heavy doors were tightly shut."

She paused and looked at me as if she wanted to make
sure that I was listening.

"Well, actually it was quite simple," she said. "Here I

was locked up with all these people whom I did not know. Many of them were kneeling. I noticed that some of them were crying on their knees, and I saw that they were praying, and they were smiling through their tears while outside the bombs were falling."

A long pause, and then, very quietly, "I had to find out what it was that made people on their knees smile under tears."

I have to say it again: she was thirteen years old when she told me this. She had found Jesus, and she had come to know quickly that he had found her. It was a union she would never leave again. In her newfound faith, I was to be her confidante and helper, but from our beginning together she understood that my Christian love had to be extended no less to her parents in the depths of their unrelieved suffering.

Her young life unfolded on a straight line. She was a radiant girl, but given to great seriousness and little laughter. The family relocated in Louisville, Kentucky; the parents struggled bravely to adjust to the new community that was so different from what they had known. Also, they felt an obligation to continue their identification with the ongoing suffering of their fellow Jews "at home." They had to share it, even if now in spirit only. That placed them beyond my reach for even the gentlest attempt to present to them their daughter's plight. They never faltered in their profound love of their only child, yet to its most urgent facet they remained adamant. "This will pass," her mother said. "She is too young to know what she wants, she is just under 'that influence.' No, with our families gassed in the concentration camps, my daughter cannot really want to become a Christian."

Young Hanna, unperturbed and loving, held on to her Savior's hand. Hers was the great gift of the Holy Spirit: with faith in the morrow to live Today. From the beginning, she saw "Jesus Only."

I did not even have to make it clear to her that my love for her, my willingness to help, would always have to be doubled, to be extended, as I have stated before, in equal measure to her parents. "You are my rock," the now-fourteen-year-old theologian said.

From time to time she went to church with me. She met the pastor. In their first conversation, his interest erupted. With and without her, we discussed her situation, prayed to be shown the way to bring enlightenment and peace to her mother with whom I visited often. Meanwhile, there were enough ways in which we could help Hanna on. The pastor suggested that I teach her Luther's Small Catechism, but she had "studied that sometime ago." The question on her mind that she repeated from time to time with a quiet urgency was, "When will I be baptized?"

"For I have come to set a man against his father, and a daughter against her mother, . . ." the Lord says. Here we were, in his name extending the hand of Christian forbearance to the smitten; here we were, in his name denying baptism to his young disciple begging for it! The miracle of it all: she understood, and she unfailingly went on loving her parents.

Late in 1942, almost on the spur of the moment, our friend, Pastor Lindsay, accepted a call from a church far away, in Arizona. He would pack up his family and leave within a few weeks. As we learned of his sudden decision, I said to Hanna, "You are losing a very good friend from sight." There were no tears, no emotions. There was this radiance shining from her eyes as she replied in her wise, never precocious, way, "I almost welcome his leaving, for now neither he nor you can deny me baptism any longer . . ."

That very moment the telephone rang. "Hanna was here," Pastor Lindsay said, his voice ringing with excitement. "Yes," I connected with him, "she is here now." "Has she told you?" he urged. "She has." I could not help whispering. "What do you think?" he wanted to know.

"I think that you and I, that we both together, will become guilty of about the gravest sin of omission if we would deny her baptism any longer," I answered. "I agree," he said.

The service took place two days later. Pastor Lindsay had asked the two leading laymen of the congregation to be witnesses and to share in the responsibility toward young Hanna and her parents in this very special situation. They pledged their discretion until the day when the parents would be able to honor their daughter's commitment.

When I arrived at the church, the pastor had prepared the baptismal font and the altar, all candles burning. We prayed together. The two men arrived; they had taken time off from their work. We tried to converse, and we waited. The principal person had not yet come. We waited some more.

Then there she was, in her brown winter coat, the blond hair wind-swept. The school books in her arm were casually deposited in a front pew; she shook hands as she greeted us.

She was ready; she faced the altar. From that moment on I remember nothing but the quiet glow of the cross in the light of the candles. I saw Jesus Only. And so, by his grace and love, did she.

At the font, my right arm was around Hanna's shoulders, my left hand as if extended to those who loved her so dearly, but could not join her on her road. The service was read; she looked straight up, then she knelt and bowed her head.

"Hanna, I baptize thee in the name of the Father, and of
the Son, and of the Holy Ghost. Amen."

We did not dwell with her on the impact of this sacred moment for which she had longed. She was to be confirmed immediately. Well versed in her knowledge about faith and doctrine, she now recited the Apostles' Creed. She was confirmed in her faith and we, her godparents, knelt with her as she made, together with us, her first communion.

She displayed no special excitement, no emotion. Now she belonged to Jesus, to Jesus Only. She radiated the certainty that all other problems now would find their proper perspective and solution.

Actually, to her there did not seem to be a real problem. She deeply regretted the lack of communication with her parents in this one point of vital importance to her, but she trusted God for the solution in his time. She was prepared for a patient wait. Her future was to be found in medicine, so she determined to study medicine. She did not look around for financial help from others: at sixteen, she secured a working permit for the Bell Telephone Company, part time, after school. A few weeks after she had begun she was promoted to work as a supervisor. She was on her way, on the strength of her faith. There were no detours, no doubts. She was gentle and kind, if at times a bit unhappy with those she loved most. She was determined, she was adamant: her Way, her Life, her Truth were Jesus Only. "This is my life," she said.

Eight years after her baptism she became a doctor of medicine. She interned in Louisville; she took her residency at Massachusetts General Hospital in Boston. I remember a conversation we had at that time, when she was thinking about specializing. "Why not general medicine," I thought out loud. "I wish more doctors would bring the Good Physician along when they sit down at the patient's bedside."

Preoccupied with her faith, she did not stop where she was. She read, she probed, she prayed. I believe it was her coming face to face with the "Catholicos" that brought her closer to Roman Catholicism. She converted, offering something like regrets to me at the possibility of hurting my feelings. I assured her of my ongoing affection, but made it clear that by her choice and decision we now were walking on different shores of a broad stream, yet still in the same direction.

I loved her as a mother loves her child. With my mind and my soul I watched her spiritual growth, the sincerity of her commitment. She saw, as I did, all answers to life, to the problems of man, in Jesus Only. I also saw that she was still searching for the place from which she could serve her Lord best.

"For I am come to set a man at variance against his father, and the daughter against her mother, and the daughter-in-law against her mother-in-law," says our Lord. "He that loveth father or mother more than me is not worthy of me: and he that loves son or daughter more than me is not worthy of me."

Our separation began. She told me that she was about to inquire about the religious life, that she hoped to enter the convent of the Medical Mission Sisters, the great order that cares for the sick and the helpless in many parts of the world. I was not surprised. She followed her Savior's guidance. As matter-of-factly as she would diagnose a patient's ailment, she would state: "I must do what I do, because I love Christ more than anything else in this world."

I found myself dead set against her intent and tried to dissuade her. I spent many hours turning to the same Lord Jesus Christ for guidance, for the violent No in my heart certainly needed clarification. The list of reasons against was too long for comfort.

The clarification came to me from our Lord. Apart from personal aspects, I was led to relive the Reformation, to give my strong and confessing Yes to Protestant, responsibly witnessing faith of the individual as opposed to the all-embracing shelter of the Roman hierarchy. I connected this to the vows she would willingly take, an act I found impossible to assent to. To me, the vow of poverty means that someone else will have to provide the unavoidable cost of living; the vow of chastity means to me to deny one's part in the Creation; the vow of obedience to me means to deny the responsibility before God of one's own mind, means a voluntary submission to authoritarian dictatorship. But more than all these things, I did not find it possible to revise my conviction: to see Jesus Only, in the comprehensive meaning of the word, means to face him in the thick of the world. To face him in diverging opinions, in hateful obstacles. To face him night and day in all the dimensions there are to life in this world, bad and good, and to depend on his redeeming grace in our Today without the safeguard of a conclave of peaceful consensus. The road "up to Jerusalem" is not well paved. It is very very rocky.

"I can serve him better this way." She said it lovingly, and she meant it.

And so I could, for my conscience' sake, accompany her no longer on her life's road. Our Lord Christ, whom by his grace we worshiped with equal fervor as best we knew, came between us. He said he would.

But not forever. You'll see.

5

GOOD FRIDAY

One step remained to be taken. It was the final, the decisive step that Jesus of Nazareth had to take to finish, in obedience to his Father's will, his mission on earth.

To reconcile man to God, that was his mission on earth. To reconcile the old Adam, man and woman alike, the mankind of the Old Testament, the mankind of Today, to God the Father Almighty, Maker of heaven and earth.

Day by day during the years of their close fellowship he had spoken to his Twelve about his mission, had gently led them to a first understanding of who he was. He had interpreted the word of God in a new sense, gauged by the Father's eternal, life-giving love for his children on earth. His fame had spread through Judea and Galilee and beyond the River Jordan into Syria. He taught his disciples, and all who came to listen, in outright statements, in gentle stories, in illustrating parables. Also, there was that mighty and unforgettable sermon by which all mankind thereafter were to live as God's own family, bound in his love.

Blending the natural and the supranatural, he had performed miracles: changing water into wine, healing the sick in body and mind, even raising the dead. He had forgiveness for the wrongdoer, comfort for the distraught, hope for the hopeless, wisdom for the narrow mind. He raised a new standard, a new maxim for living. But above all, he did what only he could do: he created faith.

Yet he did not change the darkness of man's Today to light: he was the Light that shone in the darkness. To behold him meant to see the Way; to hearken to him meant to hear the Truth; to follow him, even through the valley of the shadow of death, meant to walk in Life Everlasting.

Now the time had come for this his final, decisive step. Repeatedly he had prepared his Twelve for what was ahead for him. That he would have to suffer many things; rejected, judged, and sentenced by those who held the power; that he would be mocked and scourged and finally killed. He had not ended there, however. On the third day, he said, on the third day he would rise again . . .

How could they possibly understand that? How could they comprehend it, coming from him who had admitted to them being God's Christ? How could they grasp that this his final step was God's act of redemption from mortal sin, for them and for all mankind, to the end of time—if they believed in the man Jesus of Nazareth and followed him? And they discussed among themselves what all of this might mean, and they were glad, I am sure, that he had pledged them to secrecy. They were not to talk about these things until such time when they would really understand . . . and we with them!

And so, Jesus of Nazareth, alone among men, took the final, the decisive step to set man, captive in sin, forever free. Not in a majestic, sweeping performance revealing him as the Godhead ruling on earth, for all to see; not by setting himself apart from human kind, from his friends, his disciples with whom he lived: but by involving himself to the utmost with mortal man in his own agony and tortured death.

As he had set his face to go up to Jerusalem, so he had to set his face now from the cheering crowd that had welcomed him to the Holy City to the jeering crowd that had changed, overnight, from shouting Hosanna to shrieking, *Crucify him!*

His final step would leave behind the life-giving spirituality of his teaching, of making the Truth of God relevant to the Today, and to submit himself instead to the killing letter of the law, to all intents and purposes a means to an end in the hands of his accusers.

They were the religious leaders of their day. They were the custodians of God's truth. They were the interpreters of the Law and the Prophets: they should have been capable of recognizing the incarnate love of God, but they did not.

Instead, they were the court sitting in judgment. To them, he had to admit his true identity. But he remained silent to the indictments brought forth against him in premeditated purpose, finally to get rid of him. It meant to suffer the stubborn self-righteousness of his judges, absorbed as they were in the vanity of their minds so firmly closed to God's own promise of his Messiah, so unwilling to see the Truth established.

But amid the humiliation, the scourging and mocking, the shrieks of the mob, there was one brief moment of respite, one very small first indication of things to come. That was when Rome's governor, unsure, swaying, at least let his doubts show as he asked, "Art thou the King of the Jews?" and the already condemned man distinguished him by saying, "Thou sayest it." But, as the saying goes, "there was nothing that he could do about it" beyond, perhaps, having a plate made to be inscribed in three languages: JESUS OF NAZARETH, THE KING OF THE JEWS. It was to be put on the cross, for all to read. And Governor Pilate, in spite of himself, handed Jesus of Nazareth over to his judges, the priests, the scribes, the Pharisees, and to the howling mob for whose very sins he was about to shed his blood. He was nailed to his cross, and he died.

Toward evening the people began to rally from the exciting events of the day, even from the dread of the unleashed fury of the elements that broke loose at the hour of Jesus of Nazareth's death. When night fell over Jerusalem, one brave man went to beg the dead man's body from the Roman governor, received him, dressed his wounds, wrapped him in clean white linen, and gently laid him to rest in his own new tomb.

But the peace that prevailed in Joseph of Arimathea's tomb that night was not shared by the people of Jerusalem, we can be sure of that. There was the majority that did not want to get involved and did not care beyond the excitement of the day. But there were those closest to the Lord who were numb with grief and void of understanding all that had happened. There were also the nameless members of that agitated, rioting crowd at its worst who had jeered and mocked him up to his last moment: and in return they became the witnesses to his last words on earth, on his cross. Some of them must have begun to ponder, at least begun to ponder over it all, these events, this man's attitude, his dying, and the few words he had spoken during his ordeal!

But the chief priests and Pharisees—they at least had reason to be at rest! The law had taken its course, the rebel had gotten what he had coming. How he had irritated them, necessitating their attention, stirring them up from their comfortable day-by-day routines and, among other things, daring to bring God himself through his own person down to the level of man, speaking with authority which nobody had bestowed upon him! The agitator, the deceiver, the blasphemer. Up to the end he had given them trouble: they had to help Governor Pilate to make up his mind and pronounce the sentence! Well, it was all over; Jesus of Nazareth was dead as ordered. King Herod's son had slain the child of Bethlehem after all.

But then there was this terrible storm, and the torn

curtain in the Temple, and the murmuring of the words the dying man had spoken on the cross. To the end, he had spoken to God as his Father. "Father, into thy hands do I commit my spirit," was the last he had said before he died.

No, there was no restful sleep for the chief priests and the Pharisees that night after all. Because all of a sudden they remembered that he had said something about "rising again." No, they would take no chances. They got together, discussed it, decided what to do. When morning came, they secured Pilate's permission to seal the tomb forever, and, to make absolutely sure, they left a watch.

But no sealed tomb, no military watch, can alter God's plan, God's will for his children on earth. Jesus of Nazareth, Jesus the Christ, had fulfilled his mission on earth. Obedient to God, he had denied himself, had taken up his cross and walked, in mental anguish, in pain and agony, into the jungle of man's corruption and overcome it in his own death.

The story of Good Friday establishes the cross with all it says to us as the sign of Christ's victory over sin, over our sin. As the Wise Men saw the star and were led by it, so we may follow now the cross our Lord carries for us and dies upon so that we may live.

I thought thereon again and again in January, 1939. That was the time in my life when I had to take my one step forward, that step which meant to leave behind the life to which I was born and accustomed. It meant the people of which I was a part, it meant the responsibilities that were mine. It meant my husband, my family, my friends, and my home. It meant my position in life, my earthly possessions, and my country. It simply meant all those things which all of us have and take for granted as the years of our life go by.

Why did I have to take such drastic step? I had become an outcast in my country, at odds with its new laws. In consequence, not only my life had been forfeited, but I would also cause jeopardy of life to those nearest and dearest to me. For the association with an outcast like me was no less punishable than the outcast himself. The National Socialist ideology enforced its laws dictatorially upon us; they reached every creature living in Germany. Have you ever thought what it means, this expression "enforced its laws dictatorially"? It was very simple. By law, you had to turn on the radio. If you did not, there was always somebody who was ready to denounce you. By law, you listened. And what you heard went something like this: "For the benefit of the German people I have just enacted the following law . . ." That was the Führer. That was the atmosphere in which we lived.

As to myself—and I may repeat now some of the things you already know—I stood innocently sentenced for the accident of my birth which now made it impossible to remain by my husband's side. On the other hand, I stood gratefully guilty of having violated National Socialist legislature and its pervading spirit by being one of the founding members of the Confessing Church, that group of ministers and laymen who rallied under the cross of Christ in utter alarm when the "blood and soil"-centered ideology unmasked itself, claiming body and soul of every German man, woman, and child. It cannot be repeated often enough that it was faith in Christ that brought the Confessing Church into being; it was on the ground of that faith, on the insistence upon God's truth revealed in the Old and New Testaments as the basic, the determining directive for man's actions that the Confessing Church opposed the new ideology.

Faith in Christ means a commitment more compelling than any man-made law, with neither possibility nor desire of any compromise. If this impresses us as sounding dictatorial, then I refer with great comfort to the fact that Jesus Christ is the Lord of all things. The great "ism's" of our time are man-made ideologies, apart from the Word of God, which is Christ. The gulf between is not unbridgeable: it can be spanned by prayers. The focal point remains through the ages: Do we live and move, and have our being in Christ, or do we find the answers to life's problems in the folds of our own minds? By his grace and with his help, I had long since taken my stand. It meant very simply that I had to take that step forward, deny myself, take up my cross and follow him.

We had one good friend whom we could trust. He arranged for my escape. He was a well-known lawyer, who "for the fun of it" had chalked up the list of indictments against me. The just punishment would have amounted to ninety-eight years in Federal Penitentiary (concentration camp would have served the purpose) and the death penalty due me sixteen times, if the arm of the law had caught up with me. It is clear that my personal pain was felt severely enough not to ask what kind of value I would ascribe to my own existence at that time, yet I remained quietly resolved not to let myself be executed even once: for it is God who gives life, and God who calls it home when he so pleases and when our labor on earth is done. And careful plans were made in deep secrecy that I should escape alive and that those who had stood by me would not be identified with me and become victims of the Antichrist in my stead.

When all was arranged and the date for the final departure set, I took a brief trip from Kiel, where we lived, to Berlin to say farewell to three people who knew what was ahead of me. They were my parents and the venerable old pastor of my home church in Berlin-Grunewald, D. Dr. Hermann Priebe.

I found him in his study in the Parish House. None of us in those days made elaborate appointments over the telephone if we could help it. We knew better than that.

I remember our final visit together as if it were yesterday. For a few moments, we sat quietly. What was to be said, after all? Then he asked, "Where will you go?" "I hope to reach Sweden safely, and from there . . . I just don't know yet. I only know I can't remain there. But I shall see to it that my husband can get his divorce from there."

My old pastor and friend replied naught, for there was nothing one could say. It was one of those rare moments in life when God does all the talking.

I remember the richness of this silence. I have remained grateful to my old friend for not even venturing any spiritual counsel at that time. He rather depended upon the knowledge that this heart of mine pulsated with the lesson that had been planted there since childhood days. That lesson was where to lift my eyes for help, in whom alone to put my trust, to whom to surrender all pains and cares, and to whose hand to cling at all times, sun-filled ones as well as these that seemed indeed to lead through that famous valley of the shadow of death. And into that blessed silence that we shared Dr. Priebe finally said just this: "Go with God, my child, and don't forget that wherever on earth you will be, you will find the doors of your church wide open. Walk right in, and behind those doors you will find people, Christian people. They will stretch out their hands to you in love and in friendship for the Savior's sake. They will soon know that you, too, have come not as a stranger, but as a loving and helping friend in Christ Jesus. . . . Go with God, my child. Be not afraid, only believe!"

Almost casually he suggested that I walk across the street to take my leave from my church. That sounded good to me, and so I went in, locking the doors behind me lest I be disturbed. I sat down on the lower one of two steps leading up to that beautiful altar of ours. High above it was the life-size statue of Christ, his right hand outstretched in a blessing. And I looked about me in that house of God which had been home to me since childhood days.

My thoughts began to flow into the quiet of the empty church. I thought . . . thought back to those outstanding days in my life that I had spent there: the day of confirmation, when I was given the word to go with me through life, "Be thou faithful unto death, and I will give thee a crown of life"; and to that day of days in the life of every genuine woman, when I had knelt there by my husband's side to receive God's blessing upon our vows . . . "until death do us part . . ." There came to mind the unforgettable sermon Dr. Priebe had preached for us on the verse from Paul's letter to the Ephesians, "Walk ye as the children of light . . ." Pensively, slowly, I thought of it all, of God's infinite love and mercy, his ever-present help in need. And that peace which passes understanding, that peace which the world cannot give, by his grace filled my entire being. And in that crucial hour of my life I sat there quietly and contentedly!

Just then, something stirred behind me, behind the altar. Immediately alarmed, I had to find out what it was. All of us in those days reacted to something unexpected, to sounds coming from an unknown source. Someone might be watching, might be listening in, ready to betray a secret, ready to cause harm, serious harm. But as I looked over my shoulder, I saw the curtain at the side of the altar move, and there was Dr. Priebe. He had put on his vestments and in his hands carried those vessels, the golden plate with the Bread of Life and the chalice with the wine. He meant for me to have the best farewell I could have, the best beginning to every new step in life, the greatest privilege the redeemed of the Lord know: to hold communion with the Savior and to receive his blessing and his forgiveness.

I made haste to turn around to kneel at our altar. Spontaneously I lifted my hands in prayer to our cross up there, willing to confess even audibly to my old friend and father confessor whatever sin might have been on my mind that should be cast where it belonged. But Dr. Priebe would not let me do it. Calmly he placed those vessels upon the altar, came down to where I knelt, knelt by my side. He lifted his hands in prayer and offered for me those words he wanted to make sure were the only words I should be willing to say, the only thoughts my mind should know, and the only prayer that in humility I should be wanting to place at my Savior's feet, and therefore he said them for me:

"Father, forgive them; for they know not what they do."

And he got up and gave me communion.

I deeply treasure this story about the power of the Crucified in my life. Not because it gave me profound comfort in great personal distress, but because it involves me, and us all, with him and with what he did for us that day that we rightly call our Good Friday.

Whoever shares this story with me is a stranger to me no longer, but a friend in Christ Jesus, a laborer with me in his vineyard, and a fellow citizen in the household of God.

And whoever reads the story in the same, quiet joy in which it was put on paper knows beyond any doubt that I got up from that altar and took my one step forward. I left it all behind, and I walked on in my Savior's hand, across the waves of the Atlantic Ocean to find my new land, our blessed United States of America; yes, even those people behind the church doors, welcoming me in faith. I put my hand to the plow without looking back as best I could, witnessing to the life-giving power of Jesus Christ and Him Crucified, for me . . . and for you.

6

EASTER

In your Easter bonnet,
With all the frills upon it,
You'll be the Grandest Lady in the Easter Parade.

The happy tune to happy words—everybody knows it, everybody loves it. It enlivens the scene as festive crowds turn out for that time-honored pageant, the Easter Parade on Easter Day. Men, women, children, whole families, bedecked in brand-new finery, present themselves in that gay get-together following church services. One greets friends, exchanges pleasantries, exclaims over hats and outfits. One might even carry home a prize for being best-dressed in one of the various categories under scrutiny of a set of judges representing the neighborhood and the clothes industry.

It is spring, the dead of winter is overcome. Nature stirs to new life, and so do we. We love the new life that unfolds before our eyes. The older we get, from spring to spring it becomes more exciting—if not more thought-provoking— this watching nature come to life again after it seemed dead these long winter months! And if spring is slow in coming, we even lend a helping hand: our city's hot houses and nurseries come out with blooming bushes and plants to dress up the scene for our Easter Parade. How lovely it looks!

How lovely especially the churches in their special Easter finery. Great numbers of people go to see it. Altar and chancel with their display of flowers, the abundance of the lilies that make us think of death and life alike, of simplicity and splendor all in one breath.

Elating is the sight of the throngs of people crowding the pews with an air of expectancy amid this festive loveliness. Indeed, something very special is going on; the service is very special, the music is jubilant. It stirs the emotions, and thoughts about one's own place in all of this—does it not have to do with Life Eternal—are not at all far off. We may even find that our thoughts are met by what the preacher says from the pulpit, and in our agreement there is still more general happiness. And in heartily shared approval the great congregation joins in the singing of those triumphant words which are the real basis of all that happiness:

Jesus Christ is risen today . . .

Yes, it was lovely, we plan to attend here again next Easter. The people are friendly, the parishioners make a special effort at greeting the guests; the minister at the door shakes hands to praises of his sermon. The church empties upon the avenue or the square where the Easter Parade is forming.

It is still, very still in the church, at the altar, where those lilies still adorn the cross. So still, so gently and painfully still as it was before sunrise over Jerusalem in the small hours of the third day after Jesus of Nazareth had been crucified (with two other evildoers). The big city slept, slept through a new earthquake that rumbled but briefly, slept away from whatever happened yesterday and was now a thing of the past. It was the end of the Passover, and a big Sabbath which under the law would be a very quiet day. People would spend it at home and not engage in idle talk.

The chief priests and the elders, as the city fathers and keepers of the law, had been careful to insure that quiet of the big Sabbath now coming to its close. We know that their thoughts were still with that man from Nazareth who had said that he was God's Messiah, whom they had sentenced to die for this blasphemy accordingly.

Why would their minds retain it all? Why did they not find comfort in the knowledge that the people of Jerusalem as a whole would not care about the incident? How was it that they, the chief priests and elders, accustomed to ruling in cold blood, could not discard it from their thoughts? Had they not taken care of his pronouncement, "After three days I will rise again," by sealing the tomb and placing a watch?

Well, yes, the man was now dead beyond any doubt. His tongue was silenced, never to speak again. His hands, nailed to the cross, would perform miracles no longer and get people upset. His friends, the disciples, were nowhere to be seen. They knew it, too: his side had been pierced. He was dead, dead, dead. They were rid of him, no longer threatened by him in their established authority. And they made themselves attend to their duties on the big Sabbath.

The disciples, in contrast to the chief priests and elders, apparently did not remember this "On the third day, I shall rise again" their Lord had told them on several occasions. We read nothing about it. Was it wiped off their minds, all he had said to them concerning his death? They did not remember, at least not now. Under the tremendous shock, the impact of his death, they were hiding.

Toward the morning of the third day there had been another earthquake. A radiant light, like a lightning, was seen in the vicinity of the tomb. In that light an angel descended from heaven and approached the tomb. He broke the seal, rolled away the big stone, and sat down upon it. The guards were there to see it, but they were shaken with fear, dead with fright, unable to ward him off.

It was the women who arrived at the scene at this time. They had stood by their Lord on his cross, had tried to share the burden of his agony just by being there, by standing by him. Now they were left to their grief, their anguished thoughts, "How could this death happen?" There was no answer. The only answer they knew was to do something for the beloved dead Master.

Of course, they had to wait out the Sabbath day, one was not allowed to move about. But very early in the morning of the third day after his death on the cross, before sunrise, they went to the Garden where the tomb was. They brought sweet spices and ointment to anoint his loved form, and on the way they wondered how they would manage to get into the tomb.

To read the four accounts of Jesus Christ's resurrection is a climax in human experience to me. The four Evangelists—Matthew, Mark, Luke, and John—have recorded the story for us. It is fascinating to read and to find that the four accounts differ in detail. It is not important to consider the story of the one eyewitness above the others. The excitement of the few people who were actually at the tomb must have been tremendous, so much so that all would naturally differ in some detail, when they spoke about it.

To us who can read the story of Jesus Christ's resurrection, the differing details only enhance the simple fact in which all four accounts concur: The tomb was empty. The tomb was empty. The tomb was empty. The tomb was empty.

Now we are face to face with the manifestation of God Living with us, with his Yes to his creatures in his creation, with the reality of our salvation. Without the possession of this knowledge, I, for one, would not know how to live in the thick of our world's Today. The eternal truth, "God hath made him both Lord and Christ, this Jesus whom you have crucified" and, "There is none other name under

heaven given among men, whereby we must be saved,"
places the gist of the gospel within my rational grasp. Jesus
Christ, the Lord of all things, is the Lord over life and
destiny, over my life and my destiny, over us all. He is
Today.

By his grace, I can say this two thousand years after the
historic event in that little garden. Then, there were just the
grieving women with their tokens of love beyond death,
there were angels and the paralyzed guards and a few of
his disciples. There was even the risen Lord himself who
made himself known, to Mary first. It was the women to
whom those words were spoken as they are recorded in the
four Gospels.

Matthew: Fear not, for I know that ye seek Jesus, which
was crucified. He is not here: for he is risen, as he said.
Come, see the place where the Lord lay. And go quickly,
and tell his disciples that he is risen from the dead—

Mark: Be not affrighted. Ye seek Jesus of Nazareth,
which was crucified: he is risen; he is not here.—But go
your way, tell his disciples and Peter, that he goes before
you into Galilee: there shall ye see him, as he said unto you.

Luke: Why seek ye the living among the dead? He is not
here, but is risen: remember how he spake unto you when
he was yet in Galilee, saying, The Son of Man must be
delivered into the hands of sinful men, and be crucified, and
the third day rise again.

John: "Woman, why weepest thou? Whom seekest
thou?" Mary is asked by two angels in the empty tomb.
Blinded by tears, she turns to behold the likeness of a man
who repeats the question, "Woman, why weepest thou?"
She pours out her grief to him, not all of it, just this latest
bit: her Lord's body has vanished from the tomb. "Where
have you laid him?"—believing this man to be the gardener.
"Mary," he says gently. To Mary this is the blessed moment
when she no longer sees as if "in a mirror dimly," but face

to face. She recognizes Jesus, falls at his feet, and calls him
My Lord.

Jesus Christ is risen Today. Mary sees him, the other
women see him, the disciples see him, even at night on the
road to Emmaus. They see him, not an apparition, not a
wishful dream over the still form of his linen-wrapped
body: those bandages and the headcloth are found neatly
folded at the side of the tomb. They see him bodily res-
urrected, as he had predicted, and he speaks to them, even
scolds them a little.

The Lord is risen. The Lord is risen indeed. John has a
significant addition to the story somewhere else in his
Gospel: "When therefore he was risen from the dead, his
disciples remembered that he had said this unto them; and
they believed the Scripture, and the word which Jesus had
said."

They believed the Scripture, and the word which Jesus
had said. This verse brings relief from confusion, brings
inner rest and a sense of final acceptance to the men having
had a part in the drama. We may look at it like a rational
quod erat demonstrandum to man's probing mind. To his
spirit, it is the final curtain over death and the curtain rising
over Life Everlasting.

After Good Friday: Easter. He lives and we too shall live.

We can see those in whom the Risen Savior lives. They
are beyond the darkness of doubt, their hearts seem lighter
than those of other men, they have a sense of victory not of
this world. They have risen above the narrowness of life, of
their day, above the petty, the mean, the hateful. They have
risen above self and above fear. They live because Christ
lives. He motivates their every action. Yes, we can see those
in whom the Savior lives.

The story I want to tell as my Easter witness to the
Living God contains several such special persons. Also, the
story has, to my thinking, an Easter connotation as it tells

of a life of drifting uncertainty turned by Christ into a
new life of certainty.

The life of uncertainty: It was 1940; I was stranded in
the United States on a visitor's visa. I was stranded, because the beginning of the war in Europe made it impossible to pursue my legal immigration to Canada: I was
the owner of a German passport. I was stranded because
my source of support coming from a neutral country abroad
had suddenly gone dry due to the wartime development in
Europe; and stranded finally because a visitor's visa pre-
cludes the right to seek "gainful employment." Yet my
faith was intact; I simply lived one day at a time.

I had some new friends; I gave my physical energy to
the needs of forty-five children in a church home in North
Carolina. I cooked their meals in exchange for room and
board. It was a good life indeed, but it was lived in the
twilight of my "lawless" status. I had no rights that would
govern my freedom of movement, and even though on
God's hand, it remained yet a life of drifting, of uncertainty.

The story begins at the time when "Aunt Polly" had
been in my life for all of two months. She had heard of me,
perchance met me, took me into her heart and gave me the
key to her house all in one breath. No, she was not an
eccentric; in the contrary, she was so completely down to
earth that, seeing a person or a situation in need of help,
she would immediately set about giving it. She was a
member of one of America's prominent families. She had
been a widow for quite some time, and her children were
married and parents of growing youngsters. I see no need
to complete her name, for she was "Aunt Polly" to in-
numerable people even beyond the circle of her own family.
She was loved for the person, the friend, she was. To me she
was, and still is twenty years after her death, truly "the
most unforgettable character I have ever met."

Of those two months, I had spent two weeks with her

in her charming house in Louisville, Kentucky; then I went on, with her initial approval, to the church home in North Carolina. For the next weeks we corresponded as if lifelong friends. She began to urge me to return to her, cast my lot and develop whatever future from the sure haven of her home.

An unexpected event, a miracle, clarified all pending thoughts. The Government in Washington issued a set of regulations concerning people presently in the United States as visitors and unable to return, wherever to, on account of the war. For those who qualified, immigration quota numbers might now be available at the U.S. Consulate in Havana, Cuba, provided, of course, that they would apply in person. The regulations stipulated that the papers of such applicants had to be in perfect order, foreign documents translated and legalized. There had to be the usual affidavit signed by an American sponsor, plus six moral affidavits given by American citizens; and all of it together had to be examined by an American authority before leaving for Cuba.

The trip to Cuba had to be taken, the length of stay was not predictable: it might well extend over several months. In addition, the Cuban authorities, with whom we were good friends then, had their requirements. Among those was the posting of a $500 bond, just in case the applicant for an immigration visa to the United States would fail to get one.

This was a tall order to fill for any newcomer to this country and to many, including myself, beyond reach. I read about it and laid the paper aside.

I surveyed my blessings. I had food and shelter, was useful to my children and their home; I had a new and unique friend. My trust was with God: he would open my doors in his time. And I started to prepare some fresh vegetables for the children.

The next day there was another letter from Aunt Polly. "You must now come home," she wrote, with a check for bus fare included. "I am sure you have read about this new possibility to immigrate and this is what we should prepare now without delay: this is what we must do now."

This "what we must do now" meant three weeks of concentrated activity for her no less than for myself, as we amassed every one of the required papers. It meant visits to her bank for photostatic evidence of her financial situation which she matter-of-factly laid bare. The six moral affidavits were "oversigned" as she mentioned their need to her friends. When I meekly observed, "But, Aunt Polly, it is not you who is going to immigrate, it is I," she laughed heartily. "Never mind, my friends know what they are doing." Finally, she wrote that enormous check to serve as a bond for the Cuban authorities, handed it to me, and murmured, "Bring it safely back and be an American citizen, me gal."

During the week of the final formalities in New York with American and Cuban authorities, I had the encounter with Hanna, told in the Fourth Chapter. Enveloped in my own affairs, and constantly aware of the magnitude of Aunt Polly's actions, I was yet glad to be newly charged, at this very time, with someone else's need.

A number of people in New York warned me about the step I was about to take. "Don't go; don't leave this country," I was urged many times. "What guarantee do you have to get that immigration visa and get back in?"

"None," I smiled. "But I am going."

It is a short voyage from New York to Havana. But you can leave in icy winter and arrive in radiant summer. In between there were those hours I spent looking over the ocean, my prize possession under my arm, meaning the remarkable collection of documents called "The Affidavit." I never let it out of sight. I held on to it now, as we gently eased into port, one of the most beautiful harbors I have

seen. Would that the time be soon restored that peaceful
people may go there again, intentionally and voluntarily!

When I saw Havana for the first time, I looked up to a
radiant sky above the harbor. To the left was Morro Castle,
old, mysterious, somewhat forbidding. To our right, an
exciting view of the city with palm trees and a profusion
of flowers. Above it all, the radiance of the starlit sky.
It was unspeakably beautiful, and even my prize possession
clutched safely under my arm could not prevent me from
marveling at the creation.

The ship's passengers were put into separate categories
as we docked. Americans in evening dress were let ashore
immediately for a visit to Havana's night spots and a midnight return, for the ship would then sail back. Next were
Americans who had planned a short vacation or were part
of a cruise, and still another group made up of those who
would spend a few holiday weeks on the island.

But then there was that large group of people now herded
together on the aft deck, waiting to be allowed ashore.
Those were the homeless, the befuddled, tempest-torn,
yearning to breathe free. Yet at this moment, they
hardly had poetry on their minds. They had come to try
for an immigration visa to the United States, and they were
afraid.

I was among them, one of those anxious to secure a new
right. But I was almost ashamed of the apparent gap between us. There was a very real sense of fear over the group:
the fear of the hunted, the frustration of the outlawed.
There was the fury of the robbed, the hatred of the defense-
less, the awareness of the intense pain of inflicted suffering.
I could imagine how they felt; I knew both empathy and
sympathy, but share those feelings, I could not. I had no
fear. God was with us in the breathtaking beauty all around
us. It was not incidental, not to be ignored. It was both
comfort and encouragement; it spoke eloquently. I looked
up to the myriads of stars. I looked back upon the sea we

had safely crossed, now glittering in the moonlight; with my eyes closed I looked beyond any horizon up to God's mercy, the Father of us all here on this deck. It was Sunday, the 23d of February, 1941, the Sunday before the beginning of Lent. In the morning, I had read the epistle for the day with its climax: "But now abide Faith, Hope, Love, these three. But the greatest of these is Love." God's love. Where he is real among us, there can be no fear.

The following day was Rose Monday, a public holiday with all offices closed in Roman Catholic Cuba. A bonus day, perfect for discovering Havana. I visited the Cathedral, watched the procession. I walked through quaint old streets, enjoyed the Spanish atmosphere; I watched old men with beautiful hands shaping cigars like a piece of art. A post-card to Aunt Polly recorded the barest superlatives of joy, and gratitude, and hope. Somehow, I stopped long enough to ponder that the only load I carried was the "prize possession" underneath my left arm.

Yet somewhere along the line, somewhere in there came yet the fleeting shock, a shaking moment, "And what is going to happen if you don't succeed . . . ?" Of course it came.

Early the next morning I stood before the gate of the Consulate General of the United States of America in Havana. It was but a few minutes past opening time. "Let's not rush them too much," I decided generously and strate-gically. No one else seemed to be here yet, or so I thought. Out of the brilliant sunlight I stepped into the semidark-ness of a very large room. It was crowded with people. I was at the tail end. There was a murmuring of many voices. As my eyes adjusted, I noticed a line of people, three or four deep, inching their way toward a desk of unusually large size. A woman sat behind it who looked pleasant and friendly even over the distance. She impressed me as being all there, quite interested in what she was doing.

Obviously, this was the thing to do: I took my place in the line to surrender to her the prize possession and to hear what she would have to say.

During the long wait I felt more and more as if I was about to be asphyxiated, and not from want of fresh air. There was the same, overwhelming sense of fear hanging over that room that I had sensed the night of our arrival. Also, it became suddenly clear to me that many of the people in this room must have been around for a long time—weeks, months, who knows! And with another inner jolt it came back to me that I had been told that it might take months, that whole procedure.

When my turn had come, the secretary behind the desk had already waited on many people before me, with many more to follow. But she had still a pleasant smile for me, with a "What can I do for you?" quality to it. I gave my name and stated the nature of my business which must have startled her, I am sure. I spoke in my Sunday-best English. She stretched out her hand nonchalantly, apparently to receive the "prize possession" without any further formality. While I let go of it somewhat reluctantly, she said in flawless German, "If it makes things easier for you, we can talk together in German."

She had my heart then and there, and with it she held my life in her hands as it was contained in those documents. She perused them briefly. "All right then," she said cheerfully, as if I were the only person with the only problem in this room, "here is what you must do now. Wait around for a couple of hours. Somebody of the staff will look your papers over. It would be good to have you handy should anything require clarification. Then, tomorrow morning very early, you should go to the Cuban authorities to comply with their requirements, for your status at present is that of an immigrant to Cuba."

She mused for a moment, then continued, as an afterthought in a more personal vein: "The Cuban immigration people are said to be a bit to the tough side. Please don't get discouraged!"

I left her desk quickly, for this was now the only truly cooperative spirit I could show. Two hours later, when nothing had happened, I left for a late luncheon and pondered, back in the radiant sunshine, the experience of this morning.

The next day was Ash Wednesday. It fell on February 26. My awakening thought went to my husband across the sea from whom I was now divorced under the impact of Hitler's laws. It was his fiftieth birthday. But this was not the time for the luxury of sentimental thoughts. This was the morning I was to face those "unfriendly" Cubans and to ascertain from them the right and the permission to stay in Cuba while pursuing my real errand.

Considering the heat of the day, I dressed in a sleeveless white silk dress I used to wear when yachting with my husband. For the umpteenth time I now looked over the papers I would need "for Cuba" and convinced myself that they were in proper order.

The Cuban immigration offices were on the other side of the harbor, in a beautifully landscaped garden. I was shown to the desk of a very Latin-looking man. As I sat down, I remembered to beware of the "ugly Cuban."

"I did not know an Ash Wednesday could be so lovely," I began the conversation in an attempt to overcome some inner trepidation; also, it was impossible not to refer to the exquisite beauty of hundreds of roses visible through the wide-open French doors.

My ugly Cuban smiled. He found my papers in order. He accepted the bond and wrote a receipt. He furnished the required permit to stay in Cuba for six months, and between his Spanish-English and my German-English-Spanish we got along fine, and the work was done.

"What is next?" I asked. He left his desk, walked over to those open doors, and motioned me to wait. He was back within a few minutes, and putting a bunch of newly cut roses carefully into my hand, showed me where I had to go to get myself fingerprinted and photographed, front and both profiles, of course, and a number underneath the face—with no roses showing.

By midmorning I was back at the Consulate. The secretary and I looked at those lovely roses and enjoyed the good story. She accepted my Cuban papers, looked them over carefully, and then made what I recall sounded like a rather solemn little speech.

"If you would wait again a little while now," she began, "another hour or two, there might be questions to be asked of you. If not, please leave and go to enjoy yourself as best you can. I promise to call you as soon as there is any news. There is no need for you to inquire, and there is no way of telling you now how long it will take. But you have my promise."

I understood. I saw the numbers of people waiting with the identical errand. "I promise," I said to her with a grin, "to wait for your call, and most gratefully so!" What a woman, what a worker. I marveled at her.

No more than one hour of waiting had passed when I heard my name called. An employee of the Consulate stood in the door looking for me. The secretary motioned me to follow that man, forming the word "Questions" with her lips. A moment later I found myself in a well-furnished office opposite a young man, and on the desk before him was my prize possession.

This was an official; he was a vice-consul. An important thought flashed over my mind: "Look at the dress I am wearing . . . Here I have that fine outfit at the hotel I planned to wear for the official visit, the newly acquired gala I had named The Consul-Convincing-Dress . . ."

There was his voice. He spoke politely, with great earnestness. "Mrs. Maertens," he said, "I am somewhat puzzled. You have a very strong affidavit here, both financially and socially. It is signed by a member of one of our most prominent families. The lady is going on seventy; her affidavit is supported by her married daughter, who fully approves her mother's action. Yet it is obvious that the lady has known you in her own home for about two weeks when she wrote this affidavit."

He paused, he turned over some of those sheets, and I said nothing. To be sure, it was an incredible story. Now fear seemed to be catching up with me after all.

"Your own background justifies suspicion," he continued truthfully enough. "You are the wife of a high-ranking career officer in the German Navy. You have an unmarked German passport—" He stopped again, and the world started to spin around me.

The young vice-consul did his duty. He said that the most careful screening of immigrants was imperative, especially at this time, and, if indicated, even of the signer of the affidavit. "You must understand," he said not without kindness, "that we have to be very sure about the persons we admit now."

He wanted to say more, but it did not seem to come easily. "This is too smooth, too perfect," he finally said. "Let me make it absolutely sure: there is no relationship between this lady and yourself, by blood or by friendship, which antedates those two weeks you have spent with her at her place. And these two weeks and the ensuing correspondence sufficed to forge the apparent affection, even the sense of obligation, she has for you and causes her to sign this affidavit?" My answer, if any, was inaudible; the papers before him told the story correctly. "I am afraid," he said then, "we shall have to inquire further. This will not do . . ." And then, as an afterthought, "Unless you,

Mrs. Maertens, can help me with a plausible explanation?"

I had sat quietly, looking down upon my roses, their heads had begun to droop. Of all I had heard just now, this was the heaviest load: "You are married to a high-ranking officer . . ." How come I sat here?

But my thoughts and my feelings really did not matter. The truth did. I was asked a legitimate question to which I had to give an authentic answer. With faith in the truth, and with power greater than my own, I offered the plausible explanation:

"All my life I have believed in the Risen Savior living in people and causing them to live and act in his love. From the moment I met her, Aunt Polly has impressed me as the very incarnation of this love of my Savior Jesus Christ."

I could say no more, I had given the one and only true answer I knew. I gave it to an official of the United States of America, without knowing what manner of man he was. But he surely held my fate in his hand.

I took a deep breath. It is possible that the question "What now?" might have crossed my mind. I do not remember. I just sat there and looked at him.

He looked back, he tilted his head a little, he began to smile. Some color flushed to his cheeks. He arose and adjusted his necktie as men will do at special moments. And then, with great dignity:

"Mrs. Maertens, it gives me great pleasure to announce to you that your application for admission to the United States of America has been granted—as of this moment."

Back in the big room, minutes later, I surrendered my German passport for the coveted stamp, the immigration visa, paid my ten-dollar fee (there is always an anticlimax), thanked the secretary for her congratulations, and left what was now my Consulate General in Havana, Cuba.

Ten days later on the way home, I became friends with

an attractive woman with an intelligent face but an air of sadness. She had taken the round-trip cruise to Havana as a help in a serious marriage problem. We talked at length, hoping to ease her present pain and her dark outlook upon the future.

Shortly before New York I had to tell her that now I would have to concentrate on my own immediate future. The real act of immigration was at hand and I knew that the visa alone does not guarantee admission. The admitting officer had the final say. We shook hands and I promised to phone her once I was safely "in."

When I left the desk of the immigration officer a few hours later, with the stamp ADMITTED imprinted in my passport, there was my new friend waiting for me. She had gone ashore and returned. She laid an armful of American Beauty roses into mine and said, "Welcome to the United States of America."

At that, I heard my name paged; there was a telegram for me. "WELCOME HOME," it said. Aunt Polly, with the Risen Savior living within her, motivating her every deed, Aunt Polly had given me the United States of America.

7

PENTECOST

It is with reluctance, if not trepidation, that I begin to write the chapter on Pentecost, which is, of course, to speak of God the Holy Spirit within the context of this book. There are many reasons for such reluctance, and all of them are being brought to my consciousness by the direct influence of the very subject under discussion. If in the preceding chapter I facetiously spoke of a heavy volume of important papers clutched to my heart as my "prize possession," I now use this term in utter sincerity as I apply it to Christ's ultimate gift to us, even God the Holy Spirit. I am aware that I cannot think or write unless I ask that this very act should be his, that he should direct my thoughts and guide my pen and, in using me, allow me to serve him. Even so, the reluctance remains. It flows from awe; it stems from seeing myself clearly in my true makeup: the mortal sinner and the redeemed of Christ, blended into one, with God alive in his Creation. I should like to shout about what I have been granted to know, and I should also be happy to be most inwardly quiet about it. I should like to stand responsible in my willingness to witness to the Living God, even God the Holy Spirit; for there are also those moments when I insist that "all else," the world and all there is, are kept out of my heart and only "God and I" are together and "in."

To me, there is justification in cherishing spiritual colloquy, for the simple reason that my hunger for exchange of thought in depth finds satisfaction these days at rare occasions only. To want to talk about God, to like talking about God, to discuss present events and life itself in this perspective, to some borders on hypocrisy, to others suggests bigotry. To me, the highlight of living is found in just such conversations with a friend to whom the presence of God the Holy Spirit is as essential as it is to me. The rare beauty of being "of the same mind toward another" comes from a shared knowledge that both the dynamic power and the utter sobriety of our thinking are his gift to us.

The Nicene Creed defines him as "the Lord and Giver of Life," and later, "who spoke by the prophets." I can readily see why I should be both reluctant and willing to continue my witness to the Living God in the setting of this, my book! All right then, in His Holy Name!

Again we look to Jesus. He leads the way. After his resurrection on the day we call Easter, he continues his life on earth. For forty days he is seen again and again, and not by his disciples only. He is not seen as a spirit, but as a person of flesh and bone. He is hungry and asks for food. The disciples can touch him, speak to him, and he speaks to them. "Peace be with you," this is how he greets them as he appears in their midst. "To them he presented himself alive after his passion by many proofs, appearing to them during forty days, and speaking of the kingdom of God." We read this at the beginning of The Acts of the Apostles.

"Peace be with you": Gently he leads them through their great bewilderment caused by the things that have happened, caused also by their apparent inability to grasp all he had said and still says; caused indeed by their doubts and now by their fear of the Jews.

"Peace be with you": He begins to prepare them for

their ministry. "As the Father has sent me, even so I send you," he says.

Gone are the references to suffering and pain to be inflicted upon him. Before the crucifixion he pledged them to secrecy, not to talk about things concerning him they did not understand. Now he opens their minds to understand the Scriptures: "Thus it is written, that the Christ should suffer and on the third day rise from the dead, and that repentance and forgiveness of sins should be preached in his name to all nations, beginning from Jerusalem. You are witnesses of these things."

With them, our faith begins to take shape, receives a directive. But how does it go on? The disciples remain torn, weighing and pondering their own thoughts and emotions. Yes, they discuss what their Lord says to them among each other; they listen, but without responding; then again they are fully with him, they do understand. Still their reaction remains utterly human: they are onlookers, not participants in the story that unfolds—just this once in eternity—around them and gives them the status of participants. In effect, for the time being, they are simply sad because Jesus tells them now that he will go away "to him that sent me." "A little while, and you will see me no more; again a little while, and you will see me," he says.

By going away, by returning to the Father, he completes the circle of God's plan to save man from his sin, again in his person. In his person he carries the reconciliation of man to God the Father, the Creator. The redeemed are become one in him. And so, forty days after his resurrection and a most meaningful final part to his ministry on earth, Jesus Christ goes away. Before their very eyes, he ascends to heaven.

In him we transcend the temporal for the eternal. He is Lord over both, is the Lord of all things. In him, by his ascension, the whole Creation blends into God's everlasting Today.

By returning to the Father, he establishes the link between God's mind and man's understanding: he promises the disciples the gift of the Holy Spirit. "Behold, I send the promise of my Father upon you; but stay in the city, until you are clothed with power from on high." On several occasions he speaks with urgency: "It is to your advantage that I go away, for if I do not go away, the Counselor will not come to you; but if I go, I will send him to you. And when he comes, he will convince the world of sin and of righteousness and of judgment: of sin, because they do not believe in me; of righteousness, because I go to the Father, and you will see me no more; of judgment, because the ruler of this world is judged."

God the Holy Spirit is not an innovation. He was and is with God since the beginning. "The Spirit of God was moving over the face of the waters," we read in the opening verses of Genesis. Jesus Christ was and is with God since the beginning of time: "Before Abraham was, I AM." Jesus Christ became the Word of God to man, and still is. Jesus Christ gave the Holy Spirit of God to man, and still does, to those who believe, to those whom he chooses. The disciples were chosen, they received him. That is the story of Pentecost, the fiftieth day after Easter.

The story is recorded in the second chapter of The Acts of the Apostles. As we read it, God the Holy Spirit makes himself felt, he touches us, he moves us. Suddenly we understand. The confusion of the mind, the confounding effect of the Tower of Babel, loses its impact. We come to know the enchantment of the mind bound in God as we, his redeemed, surrender to the Holy Spirit.

He enlightens us: In radiance we behold the Eternal Truth, God—Father, Son, and Holy Spirit. He challenges us: to comprehend our God-assigned part within the Creation, within the family of God. He enables us to hear

God's voice in all things, all matters of the life of man on earth. He calls us to become aware of and face the choices we are to make throughout our life. He empowers us, the redeemed of Christ, to live and strive and act as the children of God, as friends in Christ Jesus. He makes clear to us the need of forgiveness for our failures, our sins to which we remain subject, and he helps us to mend our ways.

He grants us to know him. He grants us to be of one accord, of the same mind toward each other, in his name. He grants us spiritual sensitivity and the redeeming cry, "I believe, Lord, help thou mine unbelief." And before and above all else: He uses, guides, directs us for God's own purposes. As the disciples received him on Pentecost, so he possesses us now as even we, by his grace, possess him in our discipleship to the Lord Christ. To the redemption of our world by our Lord Jesus Christ, God the Holy Spirit, the Counselor, the Comforter, the Lord and Giver of Life, is God's own Amen.

We all use the expressions "I must get ready for Christmas" and "I must get ready for Easter," but I have never heard anybody say, "I must get ready for Pentecost." Notwithstanding the secular implication to the first two statements, it is true that many people in many lands get ready for Christmas with a fine observance of the Advent season. It is equally true that we get ready for Easter with the profound observance of those forty days before Easter called Lent. But with Easter, the climax has apparently come and gone. It seems that we are exhausted in our church life, perhaps from "too much religion," from too much emphasis on sin and repentance, if not from the simple fact of having been in church "too much."

When will we allow it to be restored to us, that wonderful truth that all things pertaining to our faith, to worship God, are never exhausting but rejuvenating and invigorating? Our faith has grown wings at the empty tomb, and now we should want to walk along with our Lord, with joyous curiosity, through those forty days after Easter up unto his ascension, then wait with the disciples for his promised gift on Pentecost. To me, the joy of those days from Easter to Pentecost underscores that the gospel, our gospel, is the Good News indeed. Jesus says, "When the Spirit of truth comes, he will guide you into all the truth." And this is the practical application, if the term be permissible: "To get ready for Pentecost" means to get ready to live our faith, and to live it Today. For we must see this clearly: without Pentecost, without the presence of God the Holy Spirit, we do not know the meaning of our faith, and we continue to live the empty life of mortal man.

The story I should like to offer in the context of this chapter is infinitely dear to me. As I set out to tell it, I am aware of the same inner reluctance of which I spoke at the beginning of this chapter. Again I know that it is God the Holy Spirit who causes this sensitivity. To hold still to it, is an immense experience in itself, but ultimately even the sensitivity has to be shared, just as this story.

My first few months in the United States as a refugee disguised as a visitor were rather void of people. To begin with, I knew a bare minimum. Also, in a measure I was numb with feeling in the face of finding myself alone with God and the United States of America. The anticlimax to the experiences of Hitler's making, which were now behind me, caused nevertheless a strange absence of the question "What now?" I was grateful for life, grateful not to hate, grateful indeed to have my expenses paid. I lived from day to day; I even owned the first lipstick of my life and enjoyed feeling wicked as I tried it out. More seriously, I lived in what I hoped was good deportment and I was waiting, unknowingly in those first few months, for God to open a door for me.

I was embarrassed about my English. I could quote Hamlet's soliloquy or Mark Antony's "Friends, Romans,

Countrymen" in nearly pure Oxford English, but it was another matter when it came to asking a waiter for a glass of water, or, asking for directions in the streets. Still worse, even if the question came off all right and was understood, there remained the horror of the reply—it always sounded Chinese to me.

But worst of all, I began to realize that at best I was making use of the language, using it as a means to an end from which I was totally detached. I recalled the incident of the last night on board of the *Gripsholm* before reaching New York. In formal dress after the Captain's dinner, I had gone up to the sun deck to watch one of nature's great spectacles: a nearly full moon shedding its light like a broad lane of silver across the dark and calm sea. In the distance, within the moonlight's path, there was an iceberg, strangely white, cold—a fascinating sight.

The man with whom I had dined and danced that night stood next to me. We had a good time together, and now we shared the extraordinary beauty before our eyes. I spoke about it with enthusiasm, maybe a little too much so; at any rate, he said facetiously, "You talk so nicely to the moon and the sea and the iceberg, can't you say something nice to me?"

Of course I could. I grinned from ear to ear and said, "Darling." He laughed hard and happy, and so did I. He was a Swede, and we both knew that I had used a word without any connotation to my mind, let alone a connection to what I might have intended to say. "Darling," here it was the equivalent of Nothing.

But when the laughter had run its course and I was at ease to draw whatever lesson from this pleasurable incident, I came up with the luxury of a newly discovered prejudice. Going for good from one land to another and from one language to another, there stood out two definitely "untranslatable" facets, or so I resolved. To love and to pray, these two things could be done in one's native tongue only.

"Darling" had proved the point. And it never entered my mind that my daily petition of those days, *"O Herr hilf, O Herr lass wohlgelingen,"* someday might be equal to "Save us, we beseech thee, O Lord! O Lord, we beseech thee, give us success!"

But then, among the matters of man nothing is as permanent as change. As I began in God's hand to discover my new life, it became obvious that I would have quite a bit of adapting to do, with language holding the highest priority. I had begun to attend a Lutheran church regularly, with services in German, so that I could pray to God! Then, in the course of the summer, a weekly study class was being offered and I went to register for it. The minister was gracious enough to talk to me about it in German. That made it easier for me to confess that I would want to attend not so much for those outlined studies on Christian fundamentals but rather as a listener, anxious to improve her English. I even asked not to participate in discussions, not to have to answer questions handed to the group. The pastor smiled and understood. "Come and make yourself at home," he said.

I had not been idle on the secular level. I attended as many movies as I could absorb, and indeed not for my entertainment. I listened and listened strenuously till the sounds would begin to make sense to my ear and reach my understanding. It was hard work. One day, there was sudden cause for great joy: upon leaving the theater I realized that I had understood the entire dialogue. I began to recapitulate the dialogue and found that it had been rather taciturn. "Me—Tarzan; You—Jane; Cheetah—Here": that was about the extent of it. Back to the class for beginners!

It was a different thing at the study group in church. I understood what was being said. Silently I thought along, without uttering a single word. Whatever the reason, was it embarrassment, was it pride, perhaps some of both? But this was the really painful part about it, and it recurred each night when we adjourned. We repeated the Lord's Prayer together. I joined in that, of course; I had memorized it some time ago. But I discovered with horror that I was repeating words, and the words meant nothing. Now I found myself in earnest dismay. My opinion that one could pray in one's native tongue only had begun to suffer uncomfortable jolts.

At that time, as I went about discovering New York, I decided to go and see Wall Street. This used to be quite a household word to Europeans, with a nimbus all its own. It is a street lined with trees on which the dollar grows; it is also paved with dollars. Back in those days it was the pulse of the world, to some at least.

The excursion began with an act of human kindness, and since kindness is a fruit of the Spirit, it shall also be recorded here. Not at all sure how to get to Wall Street, which subway system to use, I turned to a big fellow of a policeman at the corner of the street. I addressed him in the articulation of the school kid that has memorized his lesson: "Officer, I would like to go to Wall Street, please. What subway must I use? But when you answer, please speak slowly, because I am a foreigner and don't understand very much."

His blue eyes sparkled, and in his answer he substituted volume for speed. "Think nothing of it, young lady," he shouted. "We'll get that straightened out in no time!" He seized my elbow, blew his whistle, stopped the traffic on Seventh Avenue, saw me across, took me down the right steps, put a nickel into the turnstile, shuffled me through. "Remember to get off where it says Wall Street," he yelled as the express sucked me in. I never saw him again, but he lives in my heart, and I owe him a million nickels.

I reached the street at the very corner of Broadway and Wall Street. The street sign was right before my eyes. A narrow street between very tall, almost somber-looking buildings, not without dignity in appearance within a somewhat concealed air of busyness. No trees at all. Slowly I walked down the street, feeling no disappointment that I would have to do my dollar picking somewhere else. Also, the pavement consisted of ordinary, hard, unimaginative stones. Watch your step, it was in need of repair. What caught my eye, was the fleet of cars passing by, all of them of status symbol proportions. Slowly they rolled along, signs of the dignity of human accomplishment. Also, it was still B.V., Before Volkswagen.

Then I noticed people, great numbers of them. They were hurrying, somewhere, someto. I thought of little cogs in the big wheel as I looked at the passing parade. A few more steps, a few more minutes of it all, and there it was, the New York Stock Exchange.

"Ah," I thought dutifully and took a good look. Matter-of-factly, I was satisfied. With less than ten dollars in my purse I felt no immediate kinship to the building before me, but I appreciated its semiclassic features together with an awareness that I approved of capitalism after all, even if I "did not belong." But I knew of no better way how people could transact big and little business such as is necessary to keep life pulsating. But—the pulse of the world? We know better than that. The pulse of the world is God the Holy Spirit in our Lord Jesus Christ. With this belief, even Wall Street assumes its proper perspective.

I turned back to Broadway but stopped dead in my tracks. There was a church at the head of Wall Street, fitted into the gap between those towering buildings, its steeple dwarfed by its neighboring frames. It looked to me like a vision of something I wanted very much right now; but it was no vision, it was real and but a few minutes away. I had not noticed the church when I left the subway. Now the sight was a jolting surprise. Trinity Church at the head of Wall Street. I hurried toward it and entered.

"Wherever you'll go, you will find the doors of your church wide open, march right in," Dr. Priebe had said not so long ago. It rang in my heart now. The church was shrouded in semidarkness, I remember its soothing effect. My emotions were stirred as I realized that I had just made a choice, between the New York Stock Exchange and God's abode, and now I was home.

I enjoyed the rest sitting in a back pew. My eyes adjusted to the semidarkness and I noticed a constant coming and going of people. A great many were kneeling in prayer, and I noticed with amazement that most of them were men. I watched the scene with the detachment of an outsider, even though a few minutes ago I had acutely claimed being at home. I did not enjoin my prayers to those of others and therefore was outside of our common faith. I claimed my home rights, but not their obligations. The distance grew as I rested and watched, and I must confess to two unbecoming thoughts. The first: they probably lost a lot of money, was highly irreverent; the second: their prayers are not my concern, placed me next to Cain. I did not think I was my brother's keeper. My own situation suddenly became much more interesting to me. Within moments there was a good long list, a beauty of self-concern and self-pity, and after a good start this sort of thing develops without further effort. I was totally wrapped up in myself. To crown the wrong, I suddenly thought of the Lord's Prayer and lamented some more with regards to the English language.

As if hunted, I got up. With a sudden urgency, I felt the need of prayer, of an honest surrender of the pitiful self to God.

I fled the scene of the uncomfortable awakening. The little chapel to the right of the altar was empty. I stood for a while and looked without seeing. I made my way up to the little altar and knelt. I folded my hands, and I waited. "Be still, and know that I am God," it said within me, and in German.

I felt enough remorse not to tell God all my earthly woes. Didn't he know them? Didn't he allow them to happen just as right now this moment of turmoil that climaxed in thinking of the Lord's Prayer? Wasn't it his voice in all things, challenging me "what are you going to make of it?" Did I not believe that with all my heart?

And so I decided to bare to him my dismay over the "meaningless" Lord's Prayer. "Try it," the Voice said, not harshly—no, ever so gently. "Try it."

"*Vater unser*," I began. "*Vater unser, der Du bist im Himmel . . .*" No, try again. A long pause, a deep breath or two, hands folded, on my knees.

"Our Father who art in heaven—who art in heaven—" I repeated it over and over again. I began to repeat each petition, no longer quite conscious of what I was doing. I do not remember how often I said the entire prayer, but I do remember and still feel the peace that suddenly filled my heart again. I kept on, feeling a new wind blowing in my sails, moving me on unto the moment when God the Holy Spirit granted me the tremendous gift: the true transition from one language to another. Not from word to translated word, but from meaning to meaning, in intellectual and spiritual union. Confines dissolving into thin air. The Tower of Babel overcome by the life-giving, life-expanding power of God the Holy Spirit.

My new Pentecost broke forth from depths within me over which I have no control. With joy and gratitude truly not definable with words, I accepted my prize possession by surrendering to it. As it was then, so let it be now, as I write it down, with my eyes closed, led by the Spirit:

Our Father who art in heaven,
Geheiliget werde Dein Name.
Thy kingdom come, thy will be done,
Wie im Himmel, also auch auf Erden.
Give us this day our daily bread;
And forgive us our trespasses, as we forgive those who
     trespass against us;

And lead us not into temptation, but deliver us from evil.
For thine is the kingdom and the power and the glory,
   forever. Amen.

There it was, I had prayed the Lord's Prayer unaware of
the language I had used. I was elated. I left the chapel
wanting for the sunshine outside. But as I got back into
the big church, I tarried. The picture was still the same,
the semidarkness, the people kneeling in prayer. But I was
not the same. I knew again that I cared deeply about these
people. Their concerns should be, and suddenly were again,
my concerns too. I am my brother's keeper. We are God's
family. And with a newly happy heart, I took my place
among them and, led by the Spirit, enjoined my prayers to
theirs.

I remained for a long time. There was no better place
to be or to go. The semidarkness now was a good foundation for a vision of the true Light. At one point, I
reached for *The Book of Common Prayer*, Trinity Church
being an Episcopal church, and opened it at the selections
for "Pentecost, commonly called Whitsunday." And I read:

O God, who at this time didst teach the hearts of thy
faithful people, by sending to them the light of thy Holy
Spirit; Grant us by the same Spirit to have a right judgment in all things, and evermore to rejoice in his holy
comfort.

Almighty and most merciful God, grant, we beseech thee,
that by the indwelling of the Holy Spirit, we may be
enlightened and strengthened for thy service.

Send, we beseech thee, Almighty God, thy Holy Spirit into
our hearts, that he may direct and rule us according to thy
will, comfort us in all our afflictions, defend us from all
error, and lead us into all truth; through Jesus Christ our
Lord, who with thee and the same Holy Spirit liveth and
reigneth, one God, world without end. Amen.

8

TRINITY

Jesus the Christ is back with God. He no longer walks visibly among men. But now we can see him better than before: with our mind's eye, with our heart, and our soul. God the Holy Spirit, his parting gift, renders certain his eternal presence with us. God the Holy Spirit links us with him, who is one with the Father. We are now one with God, the Three-in-One, the Holy Trinity, and we have come to understand it.

"We have this treasure in earthen vessels": This quotation from Paul's second letter to the Corinthians summarizes our stand as Trinity Sunday follows Pentecost. We have this treasure in earthen vessels: the treasure, the Triune God; the earthen vessels: we.

The doctrine of the Holy Trinity was established more than sixteen hundred years ago, at the time of the first ecumenical council. It was to glorify the Triune God, Father, Son, and Holy Spirit, a logical conclusion after the revelation of Pentecost. The doctrine is man-made, but it is divinely inspired, for it sums up in man's language what our Lord himself has pronounced on many occasions.

Trinity Sunday, then, is the time to survey the whole picture, the whole mosaic of our faith, the many facts and facets that ultimately will present our faith in indelible clearness. Up to now we have learned about Jesus, about the facts and the events of his life. Now we must learn of Jesus, must listen to what he says and what he teaches. And out of both, the knowledge about him and the knowledge of him shall grow our own Christianity. Let us survey what we know.

God's manifestation of himself on earth is complete. It extended, if you will, from Christmas to the Ascension and up to Pentecost. He came to earth, he dwelt among us. He went, not back, but on to God and gave to us, as the sign of his accomplished mission, God the Holy Spirit who would link us with him forever.

Yet God's manifestation of himself on earth was not a "from—till" proposition by our standards. In the contrary, it placed man in the sphere of a circle, the circle of God's everlastingness. Safe within this circle, we face the ongoing cycle of events, God's cycle, God's events in the setting of the Today to which we are subject and with which we have to concern ourselves.

Up until now we have been onlookers picking up information about the man Jesus and his life as it unfolds within the setting of one half calendar year. We have been visitors to the scene, have even turned witness and worshiper. Our emotions were touched and stirred by what we have seen and learned. If so far we have believed, yet groping for understanding; hoped, without really knowing for what; loved, for the depth of a fine emotion, we now know that we are a part, vital to the whole story: It is for us that God did what he did. And now God charges us to see this part clearly and to accept it. There is neither vagueness nor mystery: God charges us, and on Trinity Sunday he places us squarely at the Take-it or Leave-it crossroads of our faith.

The Trinity season heads the longest season of the church year. Give or take a few weeks, it extends over one half of the calendar year. In our hemisphere, it is subject to the

heat of the summer and to vacation time for people and
pastor alike. Generally, we are used to and approve of the
great summer lull as necessary to the conduct of our lives.

Be that as it may be, but it coincides with the time of
the church year when the Christian may learn from Jesus,
listening carefully to all he says and how he says it. Conse-
quently, it is the time when the Christian redefines and
reevaluates his relationship with God and among man. This
is no small matter. It means that we attend school during
the Trinity season, God's school, our school for eternity.
If we were not too keen about going to school and delving
into the three R's when we were children, our approach is
different now. There is reward even in trying, in beginning
to try. The mind grows with joy, the heart with love, the
soul with peace. The I, the self as carrier of mind and
heart and soul, transforms the growing knowledge into
wisdom, and before us unfolds the unspeakable beauty of
the simplicity of our faith.

"We have this treasure in earthen vessels" is our motto;
the length of the Trinity season allows us to be unhurried
about this, our most important business on earth. There is
no graduation at the end of the season, there is a bit of
day-by-day graduating, as listening to the Teacher becomes
essential to us, as wanting to say Yes to God becomes the
expression of being alive and as we learn to love our faith
and live it.

To live our faith led by the Holy Spirit, we have to
remain mindful of the things we have come to know and
of our own position in God's Today. We have to be willing
to recapitulate these things over and over again in order to
keep seeing them in their right perspective. We have our
status symbol, if you will: We have this treasure, the Holy
Trinity, with us and for us and in us, who are the earthen
vessels. There is no greater wealth we can amass: this is
our faith.

We have this treasure; yet it is not ours to hoard in private ownership, to lay aside for a rainy day, or to shroud in the self-sufficient secrecy of "my own business." No, a thousand times no: Religion is not a private matter. Because of God's utterly personal relationship with each human being through his Son, we, the partners to the relationship, have to share the common gift with each other and among each other. We have to live this relationship with each other, and, if need be, even in spite of each other. Brotherhood, ordained by the Father and exemplified by the Son, is the given fact of all existence. Therefore it is in brotherhood that we survey where we stand.

Behind us are the festivals and the seasons of the church year that denote, within the span of one half calendar year, Jesus' life on earth, from his birth to his death, his resurrection and ascension. Our attention has been focussed on the events that happened to, with, and about him. With the shepherds and the Magi we bent our knees at the manger in Bethlehem. We fled with him to Egypt, there were a few bits about his youth in Nazareth and Jerusalem, about his being about "my Father's business" in the Temple at Jerusalem. From afar we have followed him through his forty days in the wilderness, being tempted, hungry, lonely. We saw his triumphant entry into Jerusalem, then his day-by-day losing favor in the eyes of the people as he stood trial. With the disciples we shared his table at the Last Supper, hearing without understanding that he was breaking to us the Bread of Life. We heard him sentenced to death for blasphemy by the custodians of the Law of God and his prophecies in cooperation with the Gentile governor of Rome.

We went, or should have gone, to Calvary and saw the crucifixion. We heard his last words, they entered our mind, and we saw him die. We hurried home for shelter, because heaven and earth opened up in an earthquake and a storm so violent that the curtain before the Holiest in the Temple was torn in half. We watched a fearless and loving man beg the scorned man's body from the authorities. We watched love undisturbed at work: Jesus of Nazareth, his wounds bound, his tortured body dressed in fair linen, was gently laid to rest in peace.

At sunrise the third day, with the women, with the disciples, even with the guards, we beheld the empty tomb. We saw the angels, they talked to us. We saw even him again, risen from the dead, alive in flesh and blood. We met him on the road to Emmaus, we found him in our midst on several occasions. We mark the pronouncedly concluding words of his ministry on earth, "For your benefit," he says, "I must return to the Father." We look, we listen, we are amazed; but in the final analysis we take in what he says without really grasping it. But then we hear him speak of God's ultimate gift of Self which he will send us. Not in body, not visible or tangible, no, more than that: the gift of reality to mind, heart, and soul: God the Holy Spirit, "who will guide you into all the truth." And he goes away as he said he would and ascends to heaven, from the land where we live to the land where we are living with him forever. And we stand waiting for the promised gift, waiting in worship and in faith, and it comes.

Yes, we do get ready for Pentecost, for the gift comes to all who believe and all whom he chooses, and now we comprehend the whole story. Comprehend that God in Christ Jesus has come to earth for our salvation. Comprehend that only by having come to know the Son we now know the Father, and that they are one. Comprehend that the final gift, God the Holy Spirit, proceeds from the Father and the Son and links us to the Godhead. He opens our understanding that we are not onlookers to a universal spectacle, but that in God's eternal order we are his foremost concern, and that we have our part in it.

Yes, we were assigned our definite part. It will never do to sit back contentedly with what we have learned about Jesus and his life. For the Lord Jesus Christ is not per se an object of our studious experience, he is the Lord of all things. He is also the second Person of the Trinity and cannot, as is so often done, be taken out of his own context, his everlasting part in the Creation, to be used by us as sweet thoughts and comfort to our woes in misdirected and misunderstood piety.

Accordingly, we must now group ourselves again in God's Today, after having recapitulated our Lord's life and ministry among us. We cannot really learn from him unless we see with utter clearness where we come in, and unless we remain willing to recapitulate this truth over and over again as it remains necessary in the course of our life.

We are the creatures of the Creator in his Creation. We are not a nameless, anonymous crowd. We, and all mankind, are Adam and Eve. We, and all mankind, are Cain and Abel. We, and all mankind, are building the Tower of Babel. There is the voice of God, but we disobey. We listen to our voice, and we kill. We try to equal God, and we fall from grace. We sin, throughout history. We sin, in his eternal Today.

But God the Father loves his creatures; he does not let go of us. He asserts himself in history, in very special events, in people. He speaks to us through his prophets: We don't take them seriously. We know better. They are unrealistic. We have our own set of values, we decide what makes sense and what not. We draw, and go on drawing, a dividing line. God on one side (unrealistic), we on the other: We just have to be realistic in our world, or so we think. From time to time we join him on his side: it feels so good. His patience is severely tested, but his love is immeasurable: he promised, again through his prophets, the Messiah, to come into the world as the Savior of all mankind.

God the Son. The Savior comes, on God's terms, not ours. God says he is his Son. Jesus says he is God's Son, is the Messiah. Ascribing glory and honor to God the Father, he manifests the truth in thought, word, and deed. But the authorities, very realistically, say No, he is not, he is a blasphemer. And we are sorry, and keep our mouth shut. The letter of the law in man's hand triumphs: the man Jesus of Nazareth is crucified on Calvary.

The grave does not hold him: he said it would not. The Risen One does not go around after the manner of man, revenging himself, humiliating or mocking those who made a mockery of him. He seeks the presence of a chosen few, those who are willing to listen, to believe, to be obedient, and to follow.

The called and the chosen: we are among them. Follow: Where? He is the Way. Where will he lead us? Into all the truth.

God the Holy Spirit: Now our innermost sensitivity responds to him. Being of Christ, he leads us into all the truth. Which truth? The truth of life, of all life. For God the Holy Spirit, the third Person of the Holy Trinity, is God's Amen to him who is the Way, and the Truth, and the Life.

We have surveyed, we have recapitulated, and in so doing have found out that the Christian never fully arrives, never may sit back in snug satisfaction: He knows that he has to recapitulate, rethink, relive the essence of his faith. He knows that he has to learn from Jesus and go on learning from Jesus, and he is glad of it.

"Teacher," a lawyer among the Pharisees asks our Lord at one time, among the many attempts to test and to trick him, "Teacher, which is the great commandment in the law?"

Jesus said to him, "You shall love the Lord your God with all your heart, and with all your soul, and with all your mind. This is the great and first commandment. And a second is like it, You shall love your neighbor as yourself. On these two commandments depend all the law and the prophets."

It should not be difficult to accept this statement as Christ's all-embracing directive for the conduct of our lives. But if we would now resolve to go right ahead and love God and our neighbor as ourselves, we would be headed for disaster: we would simply create an army of do-gooders enthusiastically carrying their bricks toward a new Tower of Babel. In secular language, we would be acting like graduates without evidence of proper learning and testing. For it is good to realize that even this, Christ's all-comprehensive directive yet remains exactly what it is: one blessed answer to just one question. Our Lord's teaching deals with all phases of existence, temporal and eternal, it is straight and clear in conception, yet intricate, better said: far-reaching in outreach and application. It cannot and should not be summarized; there are no shortcuts, no wholesale-approach: the minutest detail under sincere study develops to an additional, enriching facet of our faith. Also, Christ's work is not done nor accepted by sledge hammer: even he at times contemplated in quiet, painted in the sand before he spoke.

And suddenly, we too see it more clearly: yes, we want to rally under Christ's command. He is the only leader whose every word is eternally valid, eternally applicable to all sorts and conditions of men. Yes, we want to love God and neighbor as ourselves. We see the setting in which it has to be done. We see the hostile, confused, idolatrous world in need, in need of but one thing, the Lord Jesus Christ. This is our terrible truth, the awareness of the on-going Today that fires us to be satisfied no longer with some knowledge about that Jesus of Nazareth. Satisfied no longer with devout-routine observations as a memorial, so to speak, to the One who once walked on earth among us. Now we have to know, in detail, what he says, what he has to say, and what manner of man he is. And we study, and study some more, and we grow into his presence, and we grow in grace.

The Trinity season: we listen, we learn. Jesus Christ gives life to our life. He teaches, he preaches, he prays. His subject is God, God with man, God and man. God and man and life. He tells stories, he tells parables. To make a special point, he is careful to reduce his narrative to the level of an individual: "A certain man had two sons," "A certain man made a great supper," "There was a certain rich man," "Two men went into the Temple to pray." One by one, he heals the sick; each healing carries its special message. He points to faith in an individual and rewards it; he points to sin and says, "Repent and sin no more."

A lifetime of Trinity seasons cannot exhaust the material of our studies of Christ's teaching, his words and deeds. John says it in the last verse of his Gospel: "But there are also many other things which Jesus did; were every one of them to be written, I suppose that the world itself could not contain the books that would be written."

How true this is everybody knows who hopes to pass on even a bit of Christ's fullness to the neighbor. In growing faith we come to know that we can do so much and no more. We come to acknowledge our God-given limitations. God is endless; man is endless to God's extent. At his hand we learn that our endeavor counts, not our success. Our endeavor in his name: that is the part with which we are charged.

And it follows that, as he feeds the multitudes who follow him, he feeds even me. All he says and does, regardless to whom and where, suddenly encompasses our utterly personal relationship: it evokes my faith in him. In his ministry, not alone as it is recorded on the pages of the

New Testament, but as it conditions the charges, challenges, choices of everyday living, I know that he ministers even to me. His mind has been revealed to me; it causes me to think and gauge my thoughts to him. The simple question arises in daily choices, "Am I deciding for or against him?" There is no maybe, no in-between. But as I recognize my failures, I happily yearn for his salvation; I want to be accounted his. His love, his concern, his care, are real. To this end he lays down his life for me: he dies for me. Yet he lives again, and to the very core of all existence, of my existence, he says, "Because I live, you shall live also."

Our life, then, is in him, as he lives in us. We know it now: to live in him means to know and to accept that which he says and does. To uphold the truth that he lives in us does not mean to live like he lived: it means to live him, to live our faith. This is the faith we are to live in this world, in the full meaning of God's Today.

There is no need to dwell on what our world looks like to us today. There are too many and varying claims to descriptive accuracy. Between utter light and utter dark, there is dawn as well as dusk, there is the specter of God's rainbow. To the believer, God's Today is his own Today, no matter how involved the issues, how burning the questions. The believer knows that our Today is no worse than it has been before or will be tomorrow. To those who combine optimism with faith, there is a willingness to remain willing to give things another chance. Such persons entertain the vision that mankind is still coming. They do not close their eyes to the facts. Hordes of people everywhere still seek their own answers in gigantic killings, in the insane slaughter of wars. Man is still saturated with passion, vehemence, violence: the power of the Spirit cannot take a hold in them. How long will they need to wake up, to mature, till the day comes when they will comprehend both God and themselves?

To live our faith means to worship God. It means a quiet radiance of knowledge other than our own. It means to search after the faith that moves mountains. It means to be my brother's keeper and to love my neighbor. To live our faith means to ask God in all things, "Lord, what wilt thou have me to do?"

To live our faith means to awaken to the certainty: if the world has led wars up until today, Today it can also abolish them. If somebody says to me, "This is Utopian," I tell him that God opened the heavens when his Son came into the world and had his angels sing, "Glory to God in the highest, and on earth peace, good will toward men."

If a deeply earnest soul says to me, "We cannot accomplish peace because we can neither reach nor convince everybody on this earth," I say, "True enough, but you and I can try and begin."

For war in itself is not a big issue, it is a simple, a very small one. It is my unbridled inability, my overbearing and stubborn unwillingness to live in peace with you, my neighbor. It is my determination to enforce my mind and my power upon you. It is my disregard of Christ's healing command for forgiveness upon our antagonisms, our sins toward another. When we stop speaking, when we start taking things out on the other fellow, we have begun to kill one another off. A third person becomes involved which draws a fourth and a fifth. We are on the way; it grows like a malignant tumor, too late to stop, too late to cut out, and it devours us. Yes, we have come far in our capacity for instant and total destruction, but we still can press no button and cause a rose to bloom.

Forget about science, psychology, forget the habit and experience of millennia and turn to the simple fact: If war starts basically between "you and me," so then can peace. We are experts at making war, even though we have no directive for it. But we have the directive for peace, "I am the Way, the Truth, and the Life," he says.

But to many of us this is but a Sunday word, one out of many to which we consent in pious approval in church; then to go out, newly strengthened, so to speak, on our own "more realistic" way as conceived by psychology out of past experience, plus present accomplishment!

Dear Friends, be not misled: we are still in our Trinity season study class. The Lord himself is still our teacher. And in his holy name I dare go on saying: The Christian of the Trinity, seeking peace, seeking to end war in whatever form and variations, sits down at the conference table, big or small, domestic, national, international. He knows that Christ alone is the Way, the Truth, and the Life. There is no "yes—But" in his thinking, no special clause for special occasions. The Christian is unruffled by the fact that he has to share in discussions with others, not only not of his persuasion but opposed, if not hostile, to it. The Christian, seeking peace and ending war, does not proselytize, does not draw a dividing line by reciting his Creed: the Christian of the Trinity allows the love of God in Christ to flow through him and on. For God's love is inclusive, not exclusive: it flows whether it is accepted or not. The Christian of the Trinity is its carrier. He is fully conscious of it. This Christian knows that this love is the only remedy to wash away all sin, all ills of mankind. He knows that this love embraces all men; it embraces the addition of men and the multiplication of men. This love embraces all of mankind, for he who gives it is the Lord of all.

He is our teacher, not one of many with influence upon our life, he is the Teacher of all time. We must not tire to listen to him again and again lest we stray from him. It is very easy to stray from him. All we have to do is to accept what we learn as if it were a beautiful floral arrangement, enchanting to the eye and to our feelings. We tend it, we love it while it lasts, but lo, it begins to wilt. It is discarded; perhaps a fond memory remains and it finds its place among our thoughts on "the way of all flesh."

Yet even so, the Christian under the Trinity knows that
for every flower that wilts God causes new ones to bloom,
and he will go on doing so. For every person going out, God
sends in new ones. For every person wilting by the wayside
in apathy, two new ones should reach out, newly inspired,
as stewards of the Living God. But while there is time, our
time of our life, we learn our lessons from him. They are
not a byproduct with other lessons: they are the lesson of
life itself. We heed his words, we apply them to life as we
can reach it. To our dying breath, we apply—in his love.
The Amen to our endeavors is his, not ours.

Unrealistic? Utopia? We are forever prone to call it that.
Yet God says that he is real, is reality, is fulfillment, is
everlasting. We may as well acknowledge our "incidental
status," as we come some day and go some day. The length
of this span is his also. And while we are here, not on
borrowed but on given time, we remain his just as much
as he remains the reality of our existence. Having created
us once in his own image, he still endows us with a free
mind with which to make our choices placed before us
throughout our life. The criterion of the question remains:
Do we make our choices with him and for him; or without
him and against him?

There is (or should be) no better place to learn to make
our choices, with God and for God in all things, than our
own church. For the church is (or our church should be)
the extension of the incarnation of Jesus Christ. He built
it upon his faith in man, that man who worships him as the
Son of God. This is the rock upon which the Christian of
God's Today stands, upon which his church should stand.
This is the changeless truth of God with man (and man
with God) which renders the necessity of having to make
our choices initially a mere act of repentance and prayer.
Also, it opens the mind of the Christian of Today to face
willingly and actively the tremendous changes in our social

and economic structure and deals with them, with God.

But we shall have to begin at the bottom rung of the ladder. It is (or should be) our church where we study together at Jesus' feet, where we grow into the depth of God. I am not talking of theology; I am talking of the purpose of our church to us. It is very simple. It serves us to worship God. It serves us to learn from God, to receive his blessing upon our repentance together with his new encouragement. It serves us as our visible stronghold as we go out of its doors and apply, apply, apply God Father, Son, and Holy Spirit to all sorts and conditions of men.

No, we shall not engage now in a barrage of lamentations on the conditions of many of our churches and stir about in our grief. For there is nothing wrong with any church that is what it is meant to be: the extension of the incarnation of the Lord Jesus Christ. It is neither antiquated nor outmoded, provided it does its work: to glorify God and to take his message to man, with man willing to see it exactly this way.

For only that church fails and stumbles subsequently which has ceased to be the extension of the incarnation of our Lord. That has allowed itself to become an institution of man, consisting of weighty organizations and a business administration equal to that of a corporation. The worship services are still intact, but they are open to critical evaluation: Did you like the sermon? Did you like the music? If not, then what? Such church is bound to fall, it becomes a set of frictions, of competitive spirits, of the rule of cliques, of individualistic criticisms: in brief, an emergence of human standards are applied to God's abode. Such place is God's abode no longer. It is doomed by its own doings. The prophet Zechariah has a word for it: "What is to die, let it die." The book of Revelation has something to say to it, and we read: "You have the name of being alive, and you are dead. Awake, and strengthen what remains and is on the point of death, for I have not found your works perfect in the sight of my God. Remember then what you received and heard, keep that, and repent."

No, our church does not depend on its locality: God is everywhere. It does not depend structurally on the age of its parishioners: it depends on the faith radiated and lived by those who are there. It does not depend on the popularity of the minister: it depends on the popularity of Jesus Christ. It does not depend on the magnificence of the offered music: with the angels we sing "Glory be to God on high."

The church does not depend on the activities of the organizations: it depends on the organizations welcoming the newcomer to the work of missionary outreach. And if we, of the church, talk of apathy and point to people, we often overlook our own apathy that does not point to the brother in Christ in a profoundly meant, "Come on, be with us, you belong, you are wanted, join hands with us."

Oh, the glory of a church that discovers its own wrongs, brings them out into the open for the sake of righting them, righting them in one earnest act of repentance! It means to recognize the wrongs for what they are, to offer these wrongs up to God and then to make a new start with, through, and in God. And, "Behold, he makes all things new!"

The time has come to tell my story as witness to the Living God in the Trinity season. It is a simple story about church people under the Trinity who extended the hand of God and of people who reached out for this hand and seized it. It is the story I referred to in the Introduction of this book.

We need a little background. It was the time when the Displaced Persons Act of 1948, an act of the Congress, had been in effect for a very few years. The United States had opened the doors to a given number of additional immigrants who were classified as Displaced Persons. They were waiting in European camps for their release and for a chance to start a new life in a new country. The Government and the churches of all faith groups worked together. The churches took the responsibility for the resettlement of these hapless people in cooperation with the letter of the law. This meant that only such persons could come over as were covered by the so-called Four Assurances signed by an American sponsor.

The four assurances provided a job for the applicant which would not deprive an American. It meant safe and sanitary housing, without depriving an American of such opportunity. It meant the payment of all travel expenses for the applicant and his family from the port of arrival to the destination of their trip. It meant last, but indeed not least, that the sponsor would stand and remain responsible financially: the newcomer could not become a public charge. The responsibility extended until citizenship; in other words, over a period of at least five years. It was quite a responsibility to take on, but those who did it in good faith had no cause to regret it. Quite the contrary.

There were such people, members of a Presbyterian church near St. Louis, Missouri. They had approached me denoting their interest in this program and asking for information. I went to see them twice: first, as best I remember, I met with the president of the Women's Association and the minister; then with a skeleton group made up of all organizations of the church, the minister presiding.

I do not think they left one question unasked and I obliged as best I could. Their enthusiasm developed to decision and commitment. After a Sunday sermon on the subject, the congregation resolved to take the responsibility for a Displaced Persons family and to help them to a good new beginning in their own midst.

There was a family already in this country in need of just such outstretched hand of a whole church family. It was a Latvian Lutheran pastor with his wife and young daughter, not yet ten years old. While in the Displaced Persons camp in Germany, he had helped on many of his fellow countrymen for whom those assurances arrived from America which then made the great trip possible. He had come to know of me as I directed this work on the part of my World Service group in St. Louis. He told me that in a personal letter which arrived shortly before my time in office expired. He added his own plea; he felt the time had come that he, too, should ask for those assurances that would open the doors to a new life for him, his wife, and their child.

My time at my desk was running out. I could think of no better ending than to see it run out with a view and a hope toward the future. For a moment I folded my hands and kept very quiet. Then I reached for one of those assurance forms and filled it out properly. Then, with faith in God and man I signed my name to it, three times: first as the sponsor; then as responsible for the sponsor; and finally, validating it for church denominational headquarters. In other words, I signed as responsible for the responsible for the sponsor! I hasten to add that my job carried this authority. However, I had never made use of it in this comprehensive fashion before. I simply felt that this pastor should know now that his door was about to open. Also, I knew that suitable arrangements would be on hand by the time the little family got here.

God gave his Yes to my audacity. I was privileged to greet them upon their arrival in St. Louis and to take them to their first shelter under the roof of freedom where they could catch their breath and get used to their new environment. In order to serve again in the future, the pastor needed, of course, a good stretch of adjustment, and we had just the right place where that could be had.

This was the little family now to be entrusted to the

responsible care of the people of that Presbyterian church. They became the sponsors. From the beginning, they knew that their part in the life of their charges would span a limited time only, for the goal would have to remain: the pastor would want to be a pastor again, in God's time and wherever needed. Yet those people attended to their self-chosen task with that total sense of commitment which makes a rock out of a grain of sand.

I was asked to come out and speak to them once again. This time the entire congregation had been invited to discuss the matter in detail. As far as the four assurances were concerned: The job for the pastor was under control. There was not an American clergyman who could have gone around telling of the church in Latvia, the situation in which she found herself under Communism, or about the work of this pastor in a Displaced Persons camp.

The third assurance, referring to the cost of their transportation from New Orleans to St. Louis, was of no consequence. And the fourth assurance, regarded as a scaring handicap all over the country, was immaterial in the minds of this group: they knew in faith that such newcomers would make every effort to be independent again, to be nobody's, particularly not the public's, charge.

Remained the second assurance: adequate housing, safe and sanitary, without displacing Americans. Here some members of the group had done quite a bit of scouting about, and just when they thought they were about to be discouraged, their answer had come. They found a bit of public property with what looked like a totally run-down little shack. It turned out to have two fair-sized rooms and a bath, and places for windows and doors which were, however, absent now. But they took a good look and noted the sturdy walls of red brick, also in need of repair and restoration. So why not build up a house for those who had none? Of course it could be done. They had the foundation, and inspiration, imagination, and involvement would be their basic tools.

At that third meeting we had together, they tied up all loose ends. My part was to provide once again comprehensive information that would be helpful to a thorough understanding of the family, their situation, their background. The group decided to transform the little shack into a useful and attractive home. Some of the men signed up for bricklaying, carpentry and other technical work. The hours for such work were agreed upon among people with full-time jobs willing to give of their spare time. Amounts of money were pledged toward anticipated expenses. But to me, the climax to a wonderful meeting came when the good woman who had accepted the responsibilities of leadership and coordination faced the group and, waving a sheet of paper, made a little speech.

"Now we have come to the point of furnishing the house," she said. "I am sure we all agree that it should be complete, comfortable, and as pretty as we can make it. We need a lot of things, but don't you nourish any hopes that you can go ahead and clean out your attics now and get rid of things you no longer need. There will be no white elephants. I have here the list of things we need, including toys for the little girl. I am going to read it out point by point: we want to furnish the rooms, equip the closets, fill the shelves, and—Oh, yes, who has a good refrigerator to spare?"

When she got through, the house was complete and the prospective donors delighted. Curtains and rugs and pictures for the walls were not forgotten. And the crowning touch came last, when one member of the congregation in the plumbing business got up and happily volunteered what he had to give: a brand-new toilet.

And so our new little family came to live happily as a part of their large new family who had welcomed them in the name of the Living God. Later the family went to live in the Midwest: the pastor had received a call to serve a congregation of fellow-immigrant Latvians. As I look back over these many years, I hope that their pains have helped them to grow into the depth of God. Their rocky road was smoothed by new friends, friends in Christ Jesus, by people living under the Holy Trinity.

The Trinity season of learning and living, of learning to live: a verse comes to my mind that sums it all up for us. It is from a lovely hymn written in the past century by Samuel Preiswerk, and sung to a catching tune composed by Joseph Haydn:

> Thou tookst the path of pain and death
>   That led to majesty,
> And they that truly walk by faith
>   Must take that path with Thee.
> So be it! bring us, one and all,
> To share the glory and the gall.
> The gate Thy suffering opened wide
> Leads upward into morning-tide,
>   To morning-tide,
>   Through night to morning-tide.

(Trans. by Margaret Barclay. From *Cantata Domino*; Geneva: World's Student Christian Federation, 1957. Used by permission of WSCF.)

9

ADVENT AGAIN

We have wandered through the seasons of a church year and with it through another year of our life. Our days turn to weeks, the weeks to months, and, as we increase in years, we become more and more conscious of the swift passing of time.

As time marches on, Advent comes about again. Again we commemorate the Coming of the Lord Jesus Christ into the world in which he already is and will come again, at the end of time. Would to God that the impact of this cognition cause us to break through the staid habit of our routine observations of special dates and special events unto their real interpretation; would to God that this impact jolt us to surrender to the reality of God's Today, the Today in and with our Lord Jesus Christ.

Such breakthrough can occur indeed. It may come suddenly; it may be forceful, compelling; it may also be the result of a slow awakening to the truth of God—but it is never final. The Christian on the road of Eternal Life still faces choice after choice; his life can be gauged by them. It does not matter how long the road, how rocky, how smooth. Its milestones are made up of an ever-new personal commitment, not of a set of theories and principles.

But underneath all other choices remain these two basic choices which every person claiming the name of Christ must make and willingly repeat throughout his life. It is the choice between a life of satisfaction in self and the status quo, a life of self-centered comfort with occasional fringe benefits for others less fortunate, a life of inner detachment from man's need and the issues of our day, yet prayed over in church.

The other choice entails the simple surrender of self, of one's whole life, to God who gave it. This basic choice claims full membership in God's family. It claims to live actively in the household of faith, to stand up and be counted. We worship God, then go out and face the Today. In him alone we live and move and have our being, all of it, not some small segment only and thus prepare for his Coming—from Advent to Advent Again.

Prepare: It means to live our faith. It means the practical application of the Word of God, in us and through us, to all matters of man in this world bar none: to our personal life and all it touches upon, to our national life and all it touches upon, and to our faith life and all it touches upon— yes, especially to that.

However and alas, between those two basic choices runs a broad middle road. It is built by those who remain unaware of the challenge placed by those basic choices. We get on this road with the greatest of ease, almost automatically: by the love of tradition, the comfort of habit. It is paved with the glories of past accomplishment, void of embarrassing choices and challenges. Progress and change are not part of the luggage we carry. We walk on, unwittingly, unthinkingly, and to the delight of the devil. For as we pursue the broad road of respectable Christianity we become do-gooders at best.

Let me clarify: Is it not a common occurrence, this sudden inner urgency that tells us how much there is to be done in this world, how much we have left undone? Suddenly we are shocked as we realize how far behind we are running of the profusion of human problems; yes, we are shocked at the profusion of human problems. We never seem able to catch up, let alone get ahead of them, and we should want to accomplish that very much. We are pleased to be so needed. We take the proverbial deep breath; we "call the committee and go to work."

We look at the problem, we follow the established pattern, we find the right patch. We patch up the wrongs in this world as best we can. We do face the issues of our day and for this purpose include and consult with "related interest groups." The more problems or issues we have, the busier we search for more and more new patches for the old coat, a coat of by now so many and differing patches that its original design and fabric are more and more difficult to detect.

But before I become more specific about that "old coat," let me focus our thinking upon the small difference of gigantic scope between life on that broad middle road and our ensuing conduct, and the life of total surrender to God and our ensuing conduct. This small difference of gigantic scope is the metaphor of true Christian discipleship. In the simplest possible words: The conduct of our life on the broad middle road may be Christian by connotation but it glorifies man, draws from his brainpower and perceptive faculty, even if it still includes God by asking for his blessings, if not assistance, upon our doings.

The life of basic surrender to God glorifies God, asks for his direction, then acts, with hardly any question marks left on man's mind, for he has the Word of God. This is not theology, this is Christ's command. "Thou shalt love the Lord thy God with all thy heart and mind and soul" and—then!—"thy neighbor as thyself." This is, in fact, our basic charge to apply the Word of God—and all it entails—to all matters of man.

But in all fairness to so many good people on that middle road who believe in good faith and good will merely that "we must do the right thing" and probe no deeper, let me get back to that old coat. This old coat in need of no patches yet constantly getting them is, symbolically speaking, the love of God. He gives it to every creature he allows into being, yet leaving the choice of acceptance and use to him. This coat covers the naked shame of our first disobedience, protects the fratricide, warms the people in Noah's ark, and so on through the ages. It is ours today as it was yesterday and will be tomorrow, an invisible uniform, if you will, of the children of God. It is shared by young and old, the rich and the poor, the sinner and the just, the intelligent and the simpleminded. It is there to be shared by black and white and yellow-skinned, by Jew and Gentile, by those who are far off and those who are nigh: all have it, all may wear and be identified by it. I like to think of the coat in relationship to our Lord Christ, the incarnation of God's love: On the cross, beneath his feet, his executioners gamble over his coat and divide it; that is when the patch-work began.

But it is also the time when the call for total surrender to God rings out with compelling clearness. Our Lord's word, "It is finished," refers to his mission on earth, the salvation of man. If we hear the call and heed it, he will bear us safely home to God—home, that is where we belong and from where we act. At home with God, quite naturally we are subject to the rules of his, our eternal, home. We share its rules, we share the coat of God's love with our neighbor whose face we can see.

Yet with all our sharing, there is indeed Oneness, but there is no such thing as wholesale Christianity. God does not reach out for us in bulk; he calls each human being individually. And each human being must allow himself to be reached individually and make his happy and only choice of total surrender to God. No Christian cumulative effort, no committee, commission, consultation, or conference, yea even no congregation, will ultimately make sense unless it consists of people totally surrendered to God first, who then come to the conference, yes even the Holy Table. This is the true brotherhood of man, the only Oneness in him. The Oneness comes without effort, particularly the effort of organization: it simply is. It accepts the fellow brother as he is, not in spite of his differences of which there will always be an abundance, but because of his differences. For over and beyond the bond in God, the acceptance of differences in creative goodwill causes an emergence of fruitful progress, wherever progress must be sought and made, and wherever the doggedness of adversity should be turned into a new beginning within God's Today. And just this, this permission of an ever-new beginning in God, numbers among the Christian's outstanding privileges. And the sum total of what it means to apply the Word of God to all things in our personal life and all it touches upon is to be found in your and my thinking and acting being solely directed by the Word of God, which is Jesus Christ. He has given all the answers before we ever get around to asking our questions; yet the questions are there, and we have to deal with them, and we have the answers.

Yes, we have all answers; Jesus Christ is the answer. He is not limited for Christian usage. And as we apply him to our personal life and all it touches upon, so we (should) apply him to our national life and all it touches upon. But should this really be done?

The American citizen, endowed by his Creator with certain unalienable rights, pledges allegiance to the flag of the United States and to the republic for which it stands; one nation under God, with liberty and justice for all.

One nation under God: it springs from the concept upon which this land was founded. They were wise men who, among the various provisions that were to secure the blessings of liberty to ourselves and our posterity, ordained

a clear separation between church and state. A dividing
line between two governing bodies would insure the integrity of both. As this was laid out nearly two hundred years
ago, so it is sustained today by every responsible citizen to
whom the Constitution is the basic law of the land, to be
upheld and honored.

However, as indeed we separate church and state, we
separate man and God no more than we separate man and
state. It is the same man who worships God in church
where he is endowed by his Creator with certain unalienable
charges who serves the state with his substance of body and
mind as a law-abiding citizen. It then is the man totally
surrendered to God who serves his state in patriotic loyalty.
He certainly applies the Word of God to his national life
and all it touches upon. He is the wise and honest man
whom George Washington had in mind when he said,
"Let us raise a standard to whom the wise and honest can
repair; the rest is in the hands of God."

With all of this in mind, and very much aware of our
national scene of Today, I dare to suggest three points for
our thinking. I would state first of all that the complex
situation in which we find ourselves at this time, with all
our problems, domestic and foreign, is baleful to the extent
only that it requires and demands our united, responsible,
constructive attention. We need the willingness to heal that
which needs healing. It means not to be overcome by evil,
but to overcome evil with good.

Let us raise a standard: We must recapture the spirit of
the Declaration of Independence (sitting back and watch
plans for 1976 take shape is middle-road patchwork) and
overcome those grim moods in our land Today. Today we
must recapture the unique heritage of a country conceived
with liberty and justice for all. We must learn to live up to
a common display of national manners, or better still, of
those to the manner born.

"As governments are made and moved by man, so by men

they are ruined, too. Therefore, governments rather depend upon men than man upon government"—William Penn said that. With this in mind, with love of God and the neighbor, I envisage a new beginning of national relevancy and scope. It is the second thought I said I would offer.

I envisage a national television program presented at regular intervals to all Americans, at prime time. Asked by a representative group of people, the President of the United States should be the patron over a new kind of peaceable assembly of increasing numbers of Americans. It should be called "The White House Presents—One Nation Under God," and it should tell the story of America, her life, her people—the whole story. I can see the best minds of the land at work writing the sequences; I can see children and simple folk contributing stories and events. I can hear the songs of the South and the cowboy melodies of the West. I want this continued long enough to see people eagerly tune in and eventually awaken again to a brotherhood from sea to shining sea, one nation under God.

It should be a joy to pay for it. I can see the Congress, in unanimous approval of an undertaking to benefit all Americans, allocate the necessary funds by lawful procedure, namely, by carving out of the budgets for defense and outer space, say, one hundredth of one percent. The millions thus gained would still serve our own defense and further our outreach.

My third thought has to do with war. I am using the word as a concession to those who insist that we cannot be without. All right, then: Let us make war in our country. Let us make truly war on poverty by feeding the hungry, clothing the needy, providing shelter and warmth without red tape, without delay. Then let us proceed in that war against poverty in our midst without the use of poison gas— meaning handouts—yet with the needed weapons: true encounter with the source of the poverty, enlightenment for the stricken and for the helper alike, and with thorough education.

Let us make war on hate: Had Martin Luther King lived, had he been allowed to pursue his mission, I am sure he would have led his children of America, his children of God, into the promised land in which all of us are meant to dwell together in unity. Let us make war on hate: by stretching out both hands to two fellow compatriots in dependable love.

Let us make war on bigotry: Ignore it, ignore it but good and see how it fades away. And finally let us make war on apathy and pessimism; let us believe in that which is good and put our hand to the plow and till the soil and plant the seed we were so abundantly given. Let us become again what we are meant to be: God's children in dominion of the earth. And as we overcome the evil of poverty and race hatred and bigotry and apathy-pessimism, our ear catches on to the fullness of the sound: "Because I live, you shall also live."

Indeed we live because he lives. Indeed we live with him applied to our personal and to our national life and then, all in all, to our faith life and all it touches upon. I use the term "faith life" to denote our life over and beyond our own church communion. How dead it can be, this faith life, unless the Lord Christ is applied to it! And how wonderfully alive and growing, with him.

Out of the fullness of thought, the essential limitation: With joy and with hope I shall but tell of the growing rapprochement between the Roman Catholic and the Protestant churches, in the recent past and here where I live. It happens at many other places too; and it happens at the highest possible level between the World Council of Churches and the Vatican. How strange to think that our Lord's prayer to the Father, "that all may be one," has been heard by us all on both sides of the fence through the centuries; how wonderful to think that the fence has begun to tumble. It is on the local level that I could watch this, watch some good new beginnings in the growing encounter between Roman Catholic and Protestant church women: of this I want to tell.

There was an Advent luncheon to which the women of the Roman Catholic Archdiocese of Philadelphia had bidden. We, the guests, belonged to the Protestant organization Church Women United. But I do not think that we met as members of two great organizations. We did not even get together as representatives of certain churches. We all felt that we got together called by Christ, and we brought our respective churches along with us!

A wave of genuine warmth greeted us when we arrived. The place was decorated with great care and taste, and every one of our hostesses stretched out the hand of welcome to the guest within her reach. We were pinned with name tags—red for the hosts, green for the guests—and the thought occurred to me that now we were really standing together before God's open door, ready to pass through together.

Roman Catholic clergy shook hands with us as we entered the dining room. There were small tables only, making for good and personal conversation. We were seated, alternating green and red tags; the ensuing conversation flowed easily and naturally. There was a genuine sociability in Christ; there was indeed the presence of God the Holy Spirit.

The meal progressed and the program began—on a light note, to be sure. The master of ceremonies was a priest decidedly in a class with Bob Hope, judging by the gales of laughter that filled the festive room.

We had taken the first step: we had broken bread together. If such first step may appear trivial at first sight, it is yet the foundation upon which bigger things can grow.

There was a breathless quiet when the first of two speakers began.

He was a Roman Catholic priest, a well-known scholar and teacher. He had attended many sessions of the Second Vatican Council and could have well used his time for a matter-of-fact report within the general outline of the program. But he did something entirely different. He began by confessing to a change in Roman Catholic thinking. He spoke with care of their cognition now that for the past four hundred years his church had listened only to herself, looked only at herself, refused to consider any opinion other than her own and closed her doors hermetically to any fellowship outside her own walls. Then he gave a fascinating witness to the work of his church, but the true impact upon his listeners of the "outside church" was to be found in those opening statements which suddenly uncovered the united response, "For he is our peace, who hath made both one, and hath broken down the middle wall of partition between us!"

Any speaker following this would have no easy time. A high standard had been set: we had become involved, and the mood of spirit and of truth prevailed. The Protestant's turn had come. He too was a clergyman, a well-known scholar and teacher. He began by asserting his personal friendship with the first speaker; he referred to the work they had been doing together. And so he eliminated at the outset any thought of competition, of rivalry, or of—to put it in simple human terms—"Now let's see what I have to say!" So there they were, two clergymen, one Roman Catholic and one Protestant, friends in Christ Jesus and friends man to man, serving together and serving us, drawing us all together in that one fellowship.

The second address carried the same significant impact in its opening statements. The speaker began by confessing to the split in Protestantism, laying bare, in Protestant conciseness, the development of the split, caused and conditioned in history, by national standards, and by man's increasing use of his right to his own interpretation of the Word of God.

Both men kept us spellbound, moved us in mind, heart, and soul. My red-tag neighbor whispered kindly, "I liked yours better." I whispered back, "I liked yours better." We looked at each other with deep emotion and knew what we wanted to express. We had begun to talk together.

I came away from this meeting, and from an earlier one of which I shall speak later, with the resolve that I had no right to participate in this new dialogue unless I first stretched out my hand to "my own Rome." I wrote to Sister Miriam Paul, then in the mission field of her order in Pakistan, telling her of these events and their impact on my thinking. Her reply came as fast as airmail would do: it brought her warm and joyous affirmation of her readiness to see our relationship reestablished which, in her words, had never ceased. We have since corresponded and conversed. Last summer when she was on her way back to the United States to be near her ailing mother, I met her briefly in Amsterdam. She was dressed in secular clothes and looking very attractive, her blond hair windswept just as on that day of her baptism so many years ago. Our mutual love was intact; it came from the same source, and throughout our conversation we both held on to our shared vision of seeing "Jesus Only." We had to part, hoping for more time and more talks together later, when I had returned to the United States, too. I do look forward to them with a new joy as she now states, "No one has a corner on truth," and, "Things are not either-or; they are both!"

Yes, we have begun to talk together. One year after the meeting I have described, the green tags invited the red tags, to stay in the picture. It turned out to be another perfect day for Advent Christians as we explored our preparedness for our Lord's Coming again into this world in which he already is. We met in the lovely setting of a Presbyterian retreat house, once an elaborate family home on the outskirts of Philadelphia.

I had a small share in the day-long program: of this I want to tell. At the appointed hour during the morning, we broke up into small groups of ten persons each. Our group included four Roman Catholic women (among them one nun), and the six Protestants were members of Baptist, Episcopal, Lutheran, Methodist, and Presbyterian churches! We sat in a circle, looked upon one another, told our names and churches. I wondered if they could see my inner trepidation. I was keenly aware of my task, I did not want to fail them, I did not want to fail God. Like a drowning man I relived, in a fraction of a second, two significant incidents of my life: when, as a youngster in confirmation class, we went to Wittenberg to see the door to which Martin Luther had nailed his Ninety-five Theses which started the Reformation; then, when as a young woman in Rome I was admitted together with many other people to an audience with Pope Pius XI and, even though deeply impressed by the experience, yet found myself humming "A Mighty Fortress" (now being sung by Roman Catholics too!)—after having left the Vatican, I hasten to add.

"Into thy hands, dear Lord . . . ," this is how we began. And inwardly I went on praying: Show us the way, dear Lord. And then I felt that we were already on it. I told a little story pertaining to St. Nicholas Day, this being the very day, as I knew it in my youth in Germany, a Catholic Saint's Day, not a Protestant one. Yet all children alike would leave one shoe before the bedroom door: had you been good, St. Nicholas would surely put some goodies in there for you. We were all one in this—the trouble came much later! To this, ten persons laughed happily and in unison.

We spent this brief time together fully aware of how precious it could become to us all. We tried to talk about the possibilities, as we saw them, how the separate brethren could come together again. Having now prayed together as well as laughed, I felt my courage growing and worded a question with great care, directing it at the one nun among us. "Dare I ask," I said, "that you, dear sister, tell us something about what Catholics have against Protestants?"

She did not hestitate one moment. She was anxious to answer. A smile enhanced her face; her eyes shone warmly. "This is just the trouble," she exclaimed. "I should not have anything against Protestants because I know as good as nothing about them!"

At that, the dialogue erupted. All wanted to contribute. As we talked, we became really acquainted. We exchanged information. We spoke of our worship services; the Catholics described the Mass. It was an even and happy exchange in inquisitive mutuality. We were sharing our wealth, not accentuating our differences.

Yet we agreed that they are there; we knew their staggering height. For that reason we had decided not to touch on dogma at all as beyond our reach. But we decided to look at the work of great men in history—reformers, dogmatists, dissenters—no longer in the traditional pro or con judgment of our particular corner. We would instead learn to honor such men for their dedication to God, honor them for the sincerity of their search, for their courage, even for the pain of dissent and discordance. . . . "Here I stand, I can do no other, God help me. Amen."

We were a circle of ten people grouped around its center, our Lord Christ. Life pulsated in all we said and exchanged. We were enriched. There was one moment of common regret; that was when the dinner bell announced the end of our session.

For the last fifteen minutes we had talked about ways

in which ultimately we might find together. There was one in our group, sitting on my left, with the finely lined face of the elderly. She had been less eloquent than the rest of us but impressed me as a sensitive listener. I turned to her for her opinion: What did she think would finally bring us together again? She lifted her head and looked into distance. A fine smile deepened the golden color of her face. "Well," she said very, very slowly, "I am quite sure . . . if nothing else, it will be misery that will bring us together."

Will it really have to come to that? It is well within possibility, unless we really live the life of our faith as the Lord Christ commands us. In this I put my hope and my trust.

I have deliberately dwelt not on big topics under discussion but on small human aspects as tiny parts of important issues. There is nothing new, nothing revolutionary about great minds getting together to discuss big topics. But it is the simple human encounter on a new road that will lead up to a new day. Not what we discussed in these meetings carried the emphasis, but that we discussed and talked as freely and as happily as we did. In so doing, we certainly applied the Word of God to our faith life, and we were all the richer for it.

And so, from Advent to Advent Again, it is Jesus Christ the same yesterday, and today, and forever. But we, mortal human beings still in the flesh, had better keep on reminding ourselves in the words of Walter Russell Bowie's great hymn:

> New advent of the love of Christ
>   Shall we again refuse thee,
> Till in the night of hate and war
>   We perish as we lose thee?
> From old unfaith our souls release
>   To seek the kingdom of thy peace,
> By which alone we choose thee.

There is a final thought I wish to share. It stems from the yet most important meeting of Roman Catholics and Protestants of my experience. The former Greater Philadelphia Council of Churches in cooperation with the Archdiocese of Philadelphia had arranged a program, "The Challenge of the Vatican Council to Christian Unity." More than five hundred people from both faith groups had come; together they prayed the Lord's Prayer. From that moment on the hall reverberated a common joy, a growing enthusiasm. Truly great minds were disclosed in excellent addresses on the subject, and a panel discussed the questions subsequently posed by a fully alive audience.

The moderator of the panel officiated with skill, knowledge, and empathy. He seemed equally touched by the sincere enthusiasm we all felt in the face of a definite hope for the future. In feeling, he summed up indeed what we all felt when he spoke of our gratitude for this uniquely successful meeting, and it was only natural that he thought to cheer us on when he spoke of the joy of further study, of further search, search in the Bible, search for truth.

It was then that one of the panelists raised his hand and was immediately recognized. It was Professor Hagen Staack, the Lutheran, from Muhlenberg College.

He pointed to the Way. "Let us not make a mistake now," he smiled. "We need not search for the truth. We have the Truth. The Truth is Christ."